MW00580695

Beginning
MERN Stack
(MongoDB, Express, React, Node.js)

Greg Lim

Copyright © 2021 Greg Lim
All rights reserved.

COPYRIGHT © 2021 BY GREG LIM

ALL RIGHTS RESERVED.
NO PART OF THIS BOOK MAY BE REPRODUCED IN ANY FORM OR BY ANY ELECTRONIC OR MECHANICAL MEANS INCLUDING INFORMATION STORAGE AND RETRIEVAL SYSTEMS, WITHOUT PERMISSION IN WRITING FROM THE AUTHOR. THE ONLY EXCEPTION IS BY A REVIEWER, WHO MAY QUOTE SHORT EXCERPTS IN A REVIEW.

FIRST EDITION: JUNE 2021

Table of Contents

PREFACE..5

CHAPTER 1: INTRODUCTION 7

CHAPTER 2: MONGODB OVERVIEW 11

CHAPTER 3: SETTING UP MONGODB ATLAS CLOUD DATABASE 13

CHAPTER 4: ADDING SAMPLE DATA..19

CHAPTER 5: SETTING UP OUR NODE.JS, EXPRESS BACKEND...................21

CHAPTER 6: CREATING OUR BACKEND SERVER 27

CHAPTER 7: CREATING THE MOVIES DATA ACCESS OBJECT...................35

CHAPTER 8: CREATING THE MOVIES CONTROLLER................................41

CHAPTER 9: TESTING OUR BACKEND API 45

CHAPTER 10: LEAVING MOVIE REVIEWS 50

CHAPTER 11: TESTING THE REVIEWS API 59

CHAPTER 12: ROUTE TO GET A SINGLE MOVIE AND ITS RATINGS..........61

REACT FRONTEND 69

CHAPTER 13: INTRODUCTION TO REACT 71

CHAPTER 14: CREATE NAVIGATION HEADER BAR 79

CHAPTER 15: DEFINING OUR ROUTES 89

CHAPTER 16: MOVIEDATASERVICE: CONNECTING TO THE BACKEND 91

CHAPTER 17: MOVIESLIST COMPONENT 95

CHAPTER 18: MOVIE COMPONENT 111

CHAPTER 19: LISTING REVIEWS...117

CHAPTER 21: ADDING AND EDITING REVIEWS 125

CHAPTER 22: DELETING A REVIEW...135

CHAPTER 23: GET NEXT PAGE'S RESULTS..139

CHAPTER 24: GET NEXT PAGE'S RESULTS – SEARCH BY TITLE AND RATING **145**

CHAPTER 25: DEPLOYING BACKEND ON HEROKU **149**

CHAPTER 26: HOSTING AND DEPLOYING OUR REACT FRONTEND **155**

ABOUT THE AUTHOR **159**

PREFACE

About this book

In this book, we take you on a fun, hands-on and pragmatic journey to learning MERN stack development. You'll start building your first MERN stack app within minutes. Every chapter is written in a bite-sized manner and straight to the point as I don't want to waste your time (and most certainly mine) on the content you don't need. In the end, you will have the skills to create a Movies review app and deploy it to the Internet.

In the course of this book, we will cover:
- Chapter 1: Introduction
- Chapter 2: MongoDB Overview
- Chapter 3: Setting Up MongoDB Atlas Cloud Database
- Chapter 4: Adding Sample Data
- Chapter 5: Setting Up Our Node.js, Express Backend
- Chapter 6: Creating Our Backend Server
- Chapter 7: Creating The Movies Data Access Object
- Chapter 8: Creating The Movies Controller
- Chapter 9: Testing Our Backend API
- Chapter 10: Leaving Movie Reviews
- Chapter 11: Testing The Reviews API
- Chapter 12: Route To Get A Single Movie And Its Ratings
- Chapter 13: Introduction To React
- Chapter 14: Create Navigation Header Bar
- Chapter 15: Defining Our Routes
- Chapter 16: MovieDataService: Connecting To The Backend
- Chapter 17: MoviesList Component
- Chapter 18: Movie Component
- Chapter 19: Listing Reviews
- Chapter 21: Adding And Editing Reviews
- Chapter 22: Deleting A Review
- Chapter 23: Get Next Page's Results
- Chapter 24: Get Next Page's Results – Search By Title And Rating
- Chapter 25: Deploying Backend On Heroku
- Chapter 26: Hosting And Deploying Our React Frontend

The goal of this book is to teach you MERN stack development in a manageable way without overwhelming you. We focus only on the essentials and cover the material in a hands-on practice manner for you to code along.

Working Through This Book

This book is purposely broken down into short chapters where the development process of each chapter will center on different essential topics. The book takes a practical hands on approach to learning through practice. You learn best when you code along with the examples in the book.

Requirements

No previous knowledge on Node.js or React development is required, but you should have basic programming knowledge. It will be a helpful advantage if you could read through my <u>Node, Express book</u> and <u>React book</u> first which will provide you will better insight and deeper knowledge into the various technologies. But even if you have not done so, you should still be able to follow along.

Getting Book Updates

To receive updated versions of the book, subscribe to our mailing list by sending a mail to <u>support@i-ducate.com</u>. I try to update my books to use the latest version of software, libraries and will update the codes/content in this book. So, do subscribe to my list to receive updated copies!

Code Examples

You can obtain the source code of the completed project at www.greglim.co/p/mern.

CHAPTER 1: INTRODUCTION

Welcome to Beginning MERN Stack! This book focuses on the key tasks and concepts to get you started to learn and build MERN stack applications in a faster pace. It is designed for readers who don't need all the details about MERN at this point in the learning curve but concentrate on what you really need to know.

So what's the MERN stack? The MERN stack is a popular stack of technologies for building a modern Single Page Application. MERN stands for MongoDB, Express, React and Node.js:
- Node.js is one of the most popular server-side frameworks that allow us to execute JavaScript code in a web server.
- Express is a web application framework for Node.js which makes application development in Node easier and faster. Node and Express together form the middle-tier web server of the stack.
- MongoDB is a NoSQL database which stores data persistently in the form of collections and documents.
- React is a JavaScript frontend library to build user interfaces.

MERN is derived from the popular MEAN stack (MongoDB, Express, Angular, Node) where instead of using the Angular frontend framework, we use React. Another popular variant is the MEVN where we use Vue as the frontend. These frontends make up Single Page Applications (SPAs) which avoid reloading the page entirely and just fetches relevant portions of the page from the server to display new content.

The App We Will Be Building

We will build a Movie reviews app which lets users view and search for movies. They can also log in and post reviews on the movies (fig. 1a, 1b, 1c).

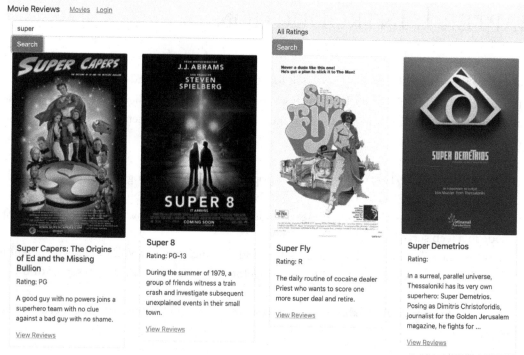

Figure 1a – Home Page with search functionality

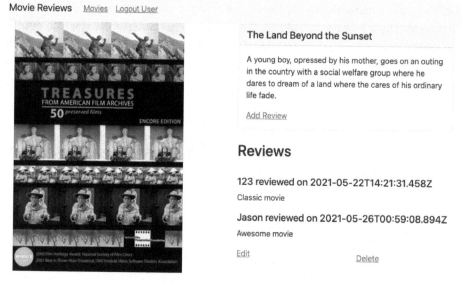

Figure 1b – Movie page listing reviews

Figure 1c — Create Review

Users can see the list of reviews in a Movie's page and post/edit/delete their own review if they are logged in. They will not be able edit/delete other's reviews though. Through this app, we will learn a lot of concepts and solidify our Node.js, Express, React and MongoDB knowledge.

We will first talk about MongoDB and how to host our database in the cloud using MongoDB Atlas. We will then create the backend of the app using Node.js and Express. Our server will interact with the database using the native MongoDB JavaScript library. After that, we will create the frontend with React and connect the frontend to the backend to complete our MERN stack app. In the last chapter, we will deploy our Node, Express backend on Heroku, and React frontend on Netlify, to run both backend and frontend in the cloud.

So, the overall structure of our app will be:
- the 'M' of the stack, MongoDB will be hosted on MongoDB Atlas
- the 'E' and 'N' , Express and Node runs the backend server (Express being part of Node) and exposes an API. Hosted on Heroku
- the 'R', React frontend calls the API and renders the user interface on the client's browser. Hosted on Netlify.

We will begin by going through the MongoDB database layer in the next chapter.

CHAPTER 2: MONGODB OVERVIEW

As indicated by the 'M' in MERN, we will use MongoDB as the backend database for our app. MongoDB is a NoSQL database. Before we talk about what is a NoSQL database, let's first talk about relational databases so that we can provide a meaningful contrast. If you have not heard of a relational database before, you can think of relational databases like spreadsheets where data is structured and each entry is generally a row in a table. Relational databases are generally controlled with SQL or Structured Query Language. Examples of popular relational databases are MySQL, SQL Server and PostgreSQL.

NoSQL databases in contrast are often called non-relational databases, where NoSQL means anything that isn't an SQL (see how it infers the popularity of SQL?). It might seem like NoSQL is a protest over SQL but it actually refers to a database not structured like a spreadsheet, i.e. less rigid than SQL databases.

The architecture of MongoDB is a NoSQL database which stores information in the form of *collections* and *documents*. MongoDB stores one or more *collections*. A *collection* represents a single entity in our app, for example in an e-commerce app, we need entities like categories, users, products. Each of these entities will be a single *collection* in our database.

If we were to map similar concepts in relational databases and MongoDB:
- a *table* in a relational database would compare to a *collection* in MongoDB.
- each row in a table (in a relational database) can be thought of as a *document* in a collection (in MongoDB).
- a *join* operation in SQL can be done with *$lookup* in MongoDB.
- instead of foreign keys, we utilize *reference* in MongoDB.

In MongoDB, a *collection* contains *documents*. A *document* is an instance of the entity containing the various relevant field values to represent the *document*. For example, a product *document* will contain title, description and price fields. Each field is a *key-value* pair e.g. `price: 26, title: "Learning Node"`.

Documents look a lot like JSON objects with various properties (though they are technically Binary JSON or BSON). An example of a *collection-document* tree is shown below:

```
Database
  → Products collection
      → Product document
          {
             price: 26,
             title: "Learning Node",
             description: "Top Notch Development book",
             expiry date: 27-3-2020
          }
      → Product document
      ...
  → Users collection
      → User document
          {
             username: "123xyz",
             contact:
                {
                   phone: "123-456-7890",
                   email: "xyz@example.com"
                }
          }
      → User document
      ...
```

You can see in the above that we have a variety of relationships. A user has a username and contact. Within contact, you have phone and email. The BSON format provides for a wide variety of support for data types like strings, integers etc.

Let's create our database in the next chapter.

CHAPTER 3: SETTING UP MONGODB ATLAS CLOUD DATABASE

The fastest and easiest way to get started with MongoDB is by using its cloud service MongoDB Atlas to host our database on the cloud. One way of setting up MongoDB is by running MongoDB on a local machine for development and testing. But MongoDB Atlas makes things a lot easier even if we are just doing a local project. Also, our entire backend and frontend will eventually be deployed to the cloud anyway.

First, sign up for a MongoDB Atlas account (https://www.mongodb.com/download-center). Under 'Deploy a free cluster', create a new account and click 'Get started free' (fig. 1).

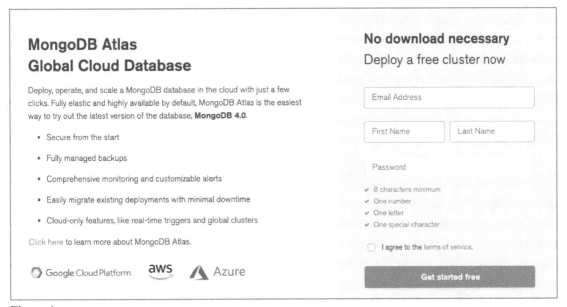

Figure 1

You will be brought to a 'Build a New Cluster' page. Under 'Global Cluster Configuration', choose 'AWS' as cloud provider (because they provide a free account without having to enter credit card details). Under 'North America', select 'North Virginia' where we can get a free tier for our MongoDB (fig. 2).

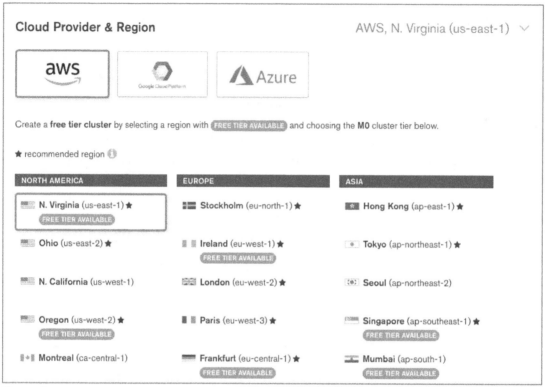

Figure 2

Next under 'Cluster Tier', choose the 'M0' free tier (fig. 3).

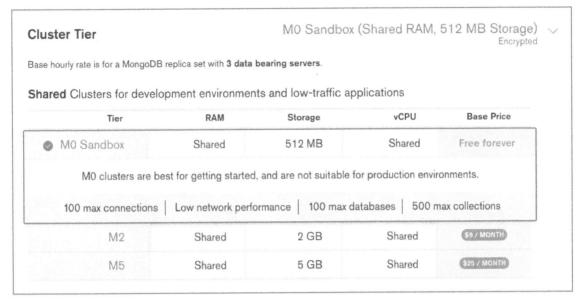

Figure 3

The good thing about Amazon AWS is that we can experiment without having to worry about making unintentional mistakes and getting a huge bill from Amazon. When your website gets more popular with more users, you can then scale up at a later stage. Keep the other default options and select 'Create Cluster.' It will prompt you saying that it takes 7-10 minutes to set up everything on AWS (fig. 4).

SANDBOX

⊶ Cluster0
Version 4.0.10

[CONNECT] [METRICS] [COLLECTIONS] [•••]

INSTANCE SIZE
M0 Sandbox (General)

REGION
AWS / N. Virginia (us-east-1)

TYPE
Replica Set - 3 nodes

LINKED STITCH APP
None Linked

Your cluster is being created

New clusters take between 7-10 minutes to provision.

Figure 4

Next, in the left panel, under 'Security', click on 'Database Access' where you do not yet have a user. Create a database user by clicking on 'Add New User' (fig. 5) and provide him with 'Read and write to any database privileges'.

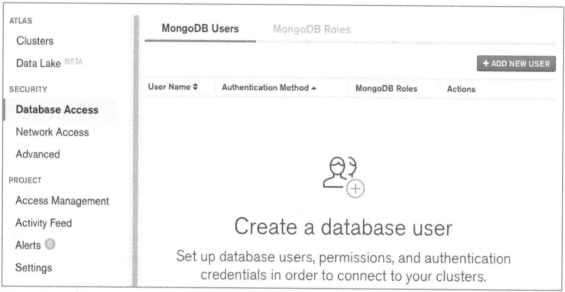

Figure 5

Next, under 'Security', 'Network Access', 'IP Whitelist', select 'Add IP Address' and choose 'allow access from anywhere' (fig. 6). This will allow our app to be accessible from anywhere in the Internet.

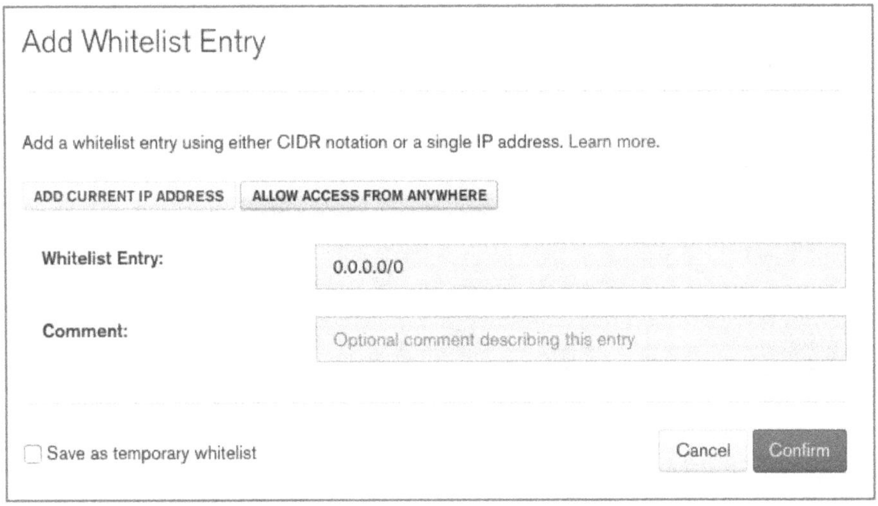

Figure 6

We will later revisit the MongoDB site to retrieve the connection string to connect MongoDB and our Node.js backend. For now, let's add some sample data to our database.

CHAPTER 4: ADDING SAMPLE DATA

One thing great about MongoDB is when you want some dummy data to try things out, you don't have to painstakingly generate your own data. MongoDB provides a lot of sample data for us. In the MongoDB Cluster, click on the three dots '...' and select 'Load sample Dataset' (fig. 1). This will load a sample dataset into your cluster.

Figure 1

To see the sample data, click on 'Collections', and you see a list of sample databases e.g. 'sample_mflix', 'sample_analytics' (fig. 2).

sample_airbnb

sample_analytics

sample_geospatial

sample_mflix

sample_restaurants

sample_supplies

sample_training

sample_weatherdata

Figure 2

In our app, we will use the 'sample_mflix' data. *sample_mflix* contains movies' data (fig. 3).

sample_airbnb

sample_analytics

sample_geospatial

sample_mflix

    comments

    movies

    reviews

    sessions

    theaters

    users

sample_restaurants

sample_supplies

```
FILTER {"filter":"example"}

QUERY RESULTS 1-20 OF MANY

  _id: ObjectId("573a1390f29313caabcd6223")
  plot: "Gwen's family is rich, but her parents
> genres: Array
  runtime: 65
> cast: Array
  title: "The Poor Little Rich Girl"
  fullplot: "Gwen's family is rich, but her pare
> languages: Array
  released: 1917-03-05T00:00:00.000+00:00
> directors: Array
> writers: Array
> awards: Object
  lastupdated: "2015-07-27 00:11:31.387000000"
  year: 1917
> imdb: Object
> countries: Array
  type: "movie"
> tomatoes: Object
```

Figure 3

For example, in the first listing, we have the 'The Poor Little Rich Girl' movie. We have the movie's runtime, title, plot, year and more. We will use these data in our app.

Having loaded our sample data, let's start creating our backend in the next chapter.

Chapter 5: Setting Up Our Node.js, Express Backend

In this chapter, we begin setting up the backend of our app with Node.js and Express. First, we will install Node.js. Go to *nodejs.org* (fig. 1) and download the appropriate version for your Operating System.

Figure 1

Installation should be straightforward. Once Node.js has been installed, go to your Terminal and run:

```
node -v
```

This shows the version of Node that you installed e.g. *v14.16.0* (at time of this book's writing).

Creating the Backend folder

In Terminal, in a location of your choice, create a folder called 'movie-reviews' e.g.:

```
mkdir movie-reviews
cd movie-reviews
```

In the *movie-reviews* folder, create a folder called 'backend':

```
mkdir backend
cd backend
```

In the *backend* folder, create a *package.json* file in the folder by running:

```
npm init
```

This will prompt a series of questions about our project (e.g. project name, author, version) to create *package.json* for us. You can of course manually create *package.json* on your own. But *npm init* saves us a bit of time when creating *package.json* files. For now, just press enter for all the questions and at the end, *package.json* (with the contents something like the below) will be generated for us.

```
{
  "name": "backend",
  "version": "1.0.0",
  "description": "",
  "main": "index.js",
  "scripts": {
    "test": "echo \"Error: no test specified\" && exit 1"
  },
  "author": "",
  "license": "ISC"
}
```

package.json contains metadata about our Node project like the name, version and its authors.

Next, install a few dependencies by running:

```
npm install express cors mongodb dotenv
```

22

As mentioned, *Express* is a framework that acts as a light layer atop the Node.js web server making it easier to develop Node.js web applications. It simplifies the APIs of Node.js, adds helpful features, helps organizes our application's functionality with middleware and routing and many others.

CORS stands for Cross-Origin Resource Sharing. By default, modern browsers don't allow frontend clients to talk to REST APIs. They block requests sent from clients to the server as a security mechanism to make sure that client-side browser JavaScript code can only talk to their own allowed server and not to some other servers which can potentially run malicious code. To circumvent this security mechanism, we can enable CORS checking, a mechanism that uses additional HTTP headers to tell browsers to give a web application running at one origin, access to selected resources from a different origin.

The *cors* package we are installing provides an Express middleware that can enable CORS with different options so we can make the right connections on the network.

The *mongodb* dependency allows us to interact with our MongoDB database.

The *dotenv* dependency loads environmental variables from the *process.env* file instead of setting environment variables on our development machine which simplifies development. We will understand this better when we create the *process.env* file later.

When installation of the above dependencies is finished, you will notice that a new property *dependencies* has been added to *package.json*.

```
{
  "name": "backend",
  "version": "1.0.0",
  "description": "",
  "main": "index.js",
  "scripts": {
    "test": "echo \"Error: no test specified\" && exit 1"
  },
  "author": "",
  "license": "ISC",
  "dependencies": {
    "cors": "^2.8.5",
    "dotenv": "^8.2.0",
    "express": "^4.17.1",
    "mongodb": "^3.6.6"
  }
}
```

Dependencies contain the dependency packages and their version numbers. For example, we have Express version 4.17.1 (at time of book's writing). Each time we install a package, *npm* saves it here to keep track of the packages used in our app.

npm install installs the specified packages into our app by fetching their latest versions and putting them in a folder called *node_modules*. Open up the *backend* folder in a code editor of your choice. In this book, I will be using Visual Studio Code (https://code.visualstudio.com/).

If you look at your app folder, the *node_modules* folder will have been created for you (fig. 2). This is where custom dependencies are saved for our project.

Figure 2

If you open and explore *node_modules*, you should be able to locate the *installed* packages. The reason why we see many other packages in *node_modules* is because our specified packages depend on these other packages and they were thus also installed. The file *package-lock.json* tracks the versions of all the dependencies of Express.

Automatic Server Restart with nodemon

Next, we will install a package called *nodemon* (https://www.npmjs.com/package/nodemon) that automatically detects code changes and restart the Node server so we don't have to manually stop and restart it whenever we make a code change. Install *nodemon* with the following command:

```
npm install -g nodemon
```

And *nodemon* will be installed globally to our system path.

CHAPTER 6: CREATING OUR BACKEND SERVER

Now, its time to create the backend server! But before we do, because we are using ES6's *import* statement, add into *package.json* the below line:

```
{
  "name": "backend",
  "version": "1.0.0",
  "description": "",
  "main": "index.js",
  "type": "module",
  "scripts": {
    "test": "echo \"Error: no test specified\" && exit 1"
  },
...
```

That will use the *import* statements from ES6.

Now, in the *backend* folder, create a new file *server.js* with the following code:

```
import express from 'express'
import cors from 'cors'
import movies from './api/movies.route.js'

const app = express()

app.use(cors())
app.use(express.json())

app.use("/api/v1/movies", movies)
app.use('*', (req,res)=>{
     res.status(404).json({error: "not found"})
})

export default app
```

Code Explanation

```
import express from 'express'
import cors from 'cors'
import movies from './api/movies.route.js'
```

We first import the *express* and *cors* middleware. We also import *movie.route.js* which is a separate file we will create later to store our routes. We then create the server with:

```
const app = express()
```

We attach the *cors* and *express.json* middleware that express will use with:

```
app.use(cors())
app.use(express.json())
```

express.json is the JSON parsing middleware to enable the server to read and accept JSON in a request's body.

Note: Middleware are functions that Express executes in the middle after the incoming request and before the output. Middlewares might make changes to the request and response objects. The *use* function registers a middleware with our Express app. With *app.use(express.json())*, the *express.json()* middleware let's us retrieve data from a request via the *body* attribute. We shall see this in code later on. Without this middleware, data retrieval would be much more difficult.

We then specify the initial routes:

```
app.use("/api/v1/movies", movies)
app.use('*', (req,res)=>{
    res.status(404).json({error: "not found"})
 })
```

The general convention for API urls is to begin it with: */api/<version number>*. And since our API is about movies, the main URL for our app will be i.e. *localhost:5000/api/v1/movies*. The subsequent specific routes are specified in the 2nd argument *movies*.

If someone tries to go to a route that doesn't exist, the wild card route *app.use('*')* returns a

404 page with the 'not found' message.

```
export default app
```

We then export *app* as a module so that other files can import it e.g. the file that accesses the database and starts the server. This allows us to separate our main server code from our database code.

Storing Environment Variables

Before we create the file that connects to the database and starts the server, we will create the *env* file to store our environment variables. Create a new file *.env*. This is where we will set the URI of our database. To get the URI, we have to go back to MongoDB Atlas. Once there, click on *connect* (fig. 1).

Figure 1

Under 'Choose a connection method', choose 'connect your application' and copy the URL (fig. 2).

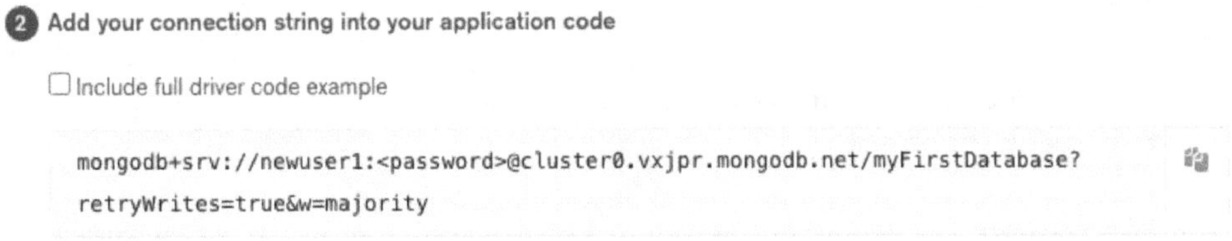

Figure 2

Go back to the *.env* file and declare a variable MOVIEREVIEWS_DB_URI and assign the copied URL to it as shown in the following code:

```
MOVIEREVIEWS_DB_URI=mongodb+srv://newuser1:pwd123@cluster0.vxjpr.mongodb.
net/sample_mflix?retryWrites=true&w=majority
```

Make sure in the connect string that you have filled in your own username (e.g. 'newuser1'), password (e.g. 'pwd123') and database name ('sample_mflix').

We will create another two variables in *.env*:

```
MOVIEREVIEWS_NS=sample_mflix // our database name
PORT=5000 // starting port of server
```

Connecting to Database and Start Server - *index.js*

Next in *backend*, create a new file *index.js*. In it, we will connect to the database and start the server. Fill in *index.js* with the following:

```
import app from './server.js'
import mongodb from "mongodb"
import dotenv from "dotenv"

async function main(){

    dotenv.config()

    const client = new mongodb.MongoClient(
      process.env.MOVIEREVIEWS_DB_URI
    )
    const port = process.env.PORT || 8000

    try {
        // Connect to the MongoDB cluster
        await client.connect()

        app.listen(port, () =>{
            console.log('server is running on port:'+port);
        })

    } catch (e) {
        console.error(e);
        process.exit(1)
    }
}

main().catch(console.error);
```

Code Explanation

```
import app from './server.js'
import mongodb from "mongodb"
import dotenv from "dotenv"
```

First, we import *app* that we have previously created and exported in *server.js*. We import *mongodb* to access our database and *dotenv* to access our environment variables.

```
async function main(){
    ...
}
```

We create an asynchronous function *main()* to connect to our MongoDB cluster and call functions that access our database.

In *main*, we call `dotenv.config()` to load in the environment variables.

```
const client = new mongodb.MongoClient(process.env.MOVIEREVIEWS_DB_URI)
```

In the above, we create an instance of *MongoClient* and pass in the database URI.

```
const port = process.env.PORT || 8000
```

We retrieve the port from our environment variable. If we can't access it, we use port 8000.

```
        await client.connect()
```

In the *try* block, we then call *client.connect* to connect to the database. *client.connect()* returns a promise. We use the *await* keyword to indicate that we block further execution until that operation has completed.

After connecting to the database and there are no errors, we then start our web server with:

```
        app.listen(port, () =>{
            console.log('server is running on port:' + port);
        })
```

app.listen starts the server and listens via the specified port. The callback function provided in the 2nd argument is executed when the server starts listening. In our case, when the server starts, it logs a

31

message 'server is running in port 5000' for example.

We wrap our calls to functions that interact with the database in a *try/catch* statement so that we handle any unexpected errors.

```
main().catch(console.error);
```

With the *main()* function implemented, we then call it and send any errors to the console.

We can then test the backend server. But first, we need to make a route.

Creating our first route

In the *backend* folder, create a new directory called *api*. In it, create a new file *movies.route.js*. We have referenced this in *server.js*. Fill it in with the following:

```
import express from 'express'

const router = express.Router() // get access to express router

router.route('/').get((req,res) => res.send('hello world'))

export default router
```

Code Explanation

movies.route.js will contain routes that different people can go to. For now, we just have one route '/' acting as a demonstration. We will add more routes later. So, if you go to *localhost:8000/api/v1/movies*, you should get a response with 'hello world'. This is because in *server.js*, we imported *movies.route.js* and specified the following path:

```
import movies from './api/movies.route.js'

...
app.use("/api/v1/movies", movies)
...
```

Thus, every route in *movies* will start with /api/v1/movies.

Running our App

In Terminal, *cd* to the *backend* directory and run *nodemon server* to test run your app and it should print out the message:

```
server is running on port:5000
```

If you didn't get any errors, it means you have successfully connected to the database (a common error is putting in a wrong password in the connection string). We are not accessing anything in the database yet, but we are at least connected to the database.

Note: You may see a deprecation warning something like:

```
"Warning: Current Server Discovery and Monitoring engine is deprecated,
and will be removed in a future version. To use the new Server Discover
and Monitoring engine, pass option { useUnifiedTopology: true } to the
MongoClient constructor."
```

It is fine to leave them there, but you can remove them by passing options to the *MongoClient*. For example, you could instantiate *MongoClient* by adding:

```
new mongodb.MongoClient(
      process.env.MOVIEREVIEWS_DB_URI,
      { useNewUrlParser: true, useUnifiedTopology: true }
)
```

See the Node.js MongoDB Driver API documentation for more information on these options.

Now, go to the browser and type in the URL *localhost:5000/api/v1/movies* and it should print out the following:

hello world

Figure 1

This shows that our route is working. And if you enter any other URL, like http://localhost:5000/123, you will get the error:

```
{"error":"not found"}
```

Which is returned by the wild card route:

```
app.use('*', (req,res)=>{
    res.status(404).json({error: "not found"})
})
```

CHAPTER 7: CREATING THE MOVIES DATA ACCESS OBJECT

Next, we will implement the movies data access object to allow our code to access movie(s) in our database. So in *backend* directory, create a directory called *dao* (data access object).

In *dao*, create the file *moviesDAO.js* with the following code:

```
let movies

export default class MoviesDAO{
    static async injectDB(conn){
        if(movies){
            return
        }
        try{
            movies = await conn.db(process.env.MOVIEREVIEWS_NS)
                        .collection('movies')
        }
        catch(e){
            console.error(`unable to connect in MoviesDAO: ${e}`)
        }
    }
}
```

Code Explanation

```
let movies
```

movies stores the reference to the database.

We then export the class *MoviesDAO* which contains an *async* method *injectDB*. *injectDB* is called as soon as the server starts and provides the database reference to *movies*.

```
        if(movies){
            return
        }
```

If the reference already exists, we return.

```
try{
    movies = await conn.db(process.env.MOVIEREVIEWS_NS)
                .collection('movies')
}
```

Else, we go ahead to connect to the database name (**process.env.MOVIEREVIEWS_NS**) and *movies* collection.

Lastly, if we fail to get the reference, we send an error message to the console.

```
catch(e){
    console.error(`unable to connect in MoviesDAO: ${e}`)
}
```

Retrieving Movies

We next define the method to get all movies from the database. Add to *moviesDAO.js* the below method:

```
static async getMovies({// default filter
    filters = null,
    page = 0,
    moviesPerPage = 20, // will only get 20 movies at once
} = {}){
    let query
    if(filters){
        if("title" in filters){
            query = { $text: { $search: filters['title']}}
        }else if("rated" in filters){
            query = { "rated": { $eq: filters['rated']}}
        }
    }

    let cursor
    try{
        cursor = await movies
                    .find(query)
```

36

```
                    .limit(moviesPerPage)
                    .skip(moviesPerPage * page)
            const moviesList = await cursor.toArray()
            const totalNumMovies = await movies.countDocuments(query)
            return {moviesList, totalNumMovies}
        }
        catch(e){
            console.error(`Unable to issue find command, ${e}`)
            return { moviesList: [], totalNumMovies: 0}
        }
    }
```

Code Explanation

```
    static async getMovies({// default filter
        filters = null,
        page = 0,
        moviesPerPage = 20, // will only get 20 movies at once
    } = {}){
```

The *getMovies* method accepts a *filter* object as its first argument. The default filter has no filters, retrieves results at page 0 and retrieves 20 movies per page. In our app, we provide filtering results by movie title "title" and movie rating "rated" (e.g. 'G', 'PG,' 'R'). So a *filters* object might look something like:

```
{
  title: "dragon", // search titles with 'dragon' in it
  rated: "G" // search ratings with 'G'
}
```

With the *filters* object, we then construct our query:

```
        if(filters){
            if(filters.hasOwnProperty('title')){
                query = { $text: { $search: filters['title']}}
            }else if(filters.hasOwnProperty('rated')){ /
                query = { "rated": filters['rated']}
            }
        }
```

We have a *query* variable which will be empty unless a user specifies filters in his retrieval, in which case we will put together a query. We first check if the *filters* object contains the property *title* with

37

`filters.hasOwnProperty('title')`. If so, we use the *$text* query operator together with *$search* to search for movie titles containing the user specified search terms. *$text* also allows us to query using multiple words by separating your words with spaces to query for documents that match any of the search terms (logical OR). E.g. "kill dragon". You can find out more about *$text* at: https://docs.mongodb.com/drivers/node/fundamentals/crud/read-operations/text/ Importantly, we also have to later specify in MongoDB Atlas that we want to enable text searches on the *title* field. We will get to that later.

Queries are very powerful in MongoDB. We have showed the *$text* operator. In the next filter where we check if user has specified the *rated* filter, we check if the user specified value is equal to the value in the database field `query = { "rated": filters['rated']}`.

```
let cursor
try{
    cursor = await movies
                .find(query)
                .limit(moviesPerPage)
                .skip(moviesPerPage * page)
    const moviesList = await cursor.toArray()
    const totalNumMovies = await movies.countDocuments(query)
    return {moviesList, totalNumMovies}

}
catch(e){
    console.error(`Unable to issue find command, ${e}`)
    return { moviesList: [], totalNumMovies: 0}
}
```

We then find all movies that fit our query and assign it to a *cursor*. If there is any error, we just return an empty *moviesList* and *totalNumMovies* to be 0.

Now, why do we need a cursor? Because our query can potentially match very large sets of documents, a cursor fetches these documents in batches to reduce both memory consumption and network bandwidth usage. Cursors are highly configurable and offer multiple interaction paradigms for different use cases. For example, we used the cursor's *limit* method to cap the number of documents returned as specified in *moviesPerPage*.

Additionally, we use the *skip* method together with *limit*. When *skip* and *limit* is used together, the *skip* applies first and the *limit* only applies to the documents left over after the skip.

This allows us to implement pagination later on in the frontend because we can retrieve a specific page's result. For e.g. if the specific page is 1, we skip 20 results first (`moviesPerPage * 1`) and then retrieve the next 20 results. If the specified page is 2, we skip 40 results (`moviesPerPage * 2`) and then retrieve the next 20 results.

```
const totalNumMovies = await movies.countDocuments(query)
```

We then get the total number of movies by counting the number of documents in the query and return *moviesList* and *totalNumMovies* in an object.

Initialising MoviesDAO

In *index.js*, add the below to import and get the reference to the *moviesDAO* file.

```
import app from './server.js'
import mongodb from "mongodb"
import dotenv from "dotenv"
import MoviesDAO from './dao/moviesDAO.js'
```

Next, add the line below:

```
async function main(){
    ...
    try {
        await client.connect()
        await MoviesDAO.injectDB(client)

        app.listen(port, () =>{
            console.log('server is running on port:'+port);
        })
    }
    ...
```

What this does is right after connecting to the database and just before we start the server, we call *injectDB* to get our initial reference to the *movies* collection in the database. In the next chapter, we will create *MoviesController* to access *MoviesDAO*.

CHAPTER 8: CREATING THE MOVIES CONTROLLER

Next, we will create the movies controller that the route file will use to access the *dao* file. In the *api* folder, create a new file *movies.controller.js* with the following code:

```
import MoviesDAO from '../dao/moviesDAO.js'

export default class MoviesController{

    static async apiGetMovies(req,res,next){
        const moviesPerPage = req.query.moviesPerPage ?
parseInt(req.query.moviesPerPage) : 20
        const page = req.query.page ? parseInt(req.query.page) : 0

        let filters = {}
        if(req.query.rated){
            filters.rated = req.query.rated
        }
        else if(req.query.title){
            filters.title = req.query.title
        }

        const { moviesList, totalNumMovies } = await
MoviesDAO.getMovies({filters, page, moviesPerPage})

        let response ={
            movies: moviesList,
            page: page,
            filters: filters,
            entries_per_page: moviesPerPage,
            total_results: totalNumMovies,
        }
        res.json(response)
    }
}
```

Code Explanation

```
import MoviesDAO from '../dao/moviesDAO.js'
```

We first import the DAO.

```
    static async apiGetMovies(req,res,next){
        const moviesPerPage = req.query.moviesPerPage ?
parseInt(req.query.moviesPerPage) : 20
        const page = req.query.page ? parseInt(req.query.page) : 0
```

When *apiGetMovies* is called via a URL, there will be a query string in the response object *(req.query)* where certain filter parameters might be specified and passed in through key-value pairs. For e.g. we have a URL:

http://localhost:5000/api/v1/movies?title=dragon&moviesPerPage=15&page=0

req.query would return the following JavaScript object after the query string is parsed:
```
{
  title: "dragon",
  moviesPerPage:"15",
  page: "0"
}
```

This is an example of what a query string look like. Later on when we can get our app running, you will get a more complete picture.

One of the query strings is *moviesPerPage*.

```
const moviesPerPage = req.query.moviesPerPage ?
parseInt(req.query.moviesPerPage) : 20
```

We check if *moviesPerPage* exists, parse it into an integer. We do the same for the *page* query string.

```
        let filters = {}
```

We then start with an empty *filters* object, i.e. no filters are applied at first.

```
if(req.query.rated){
    filters.rated = req.query.rated
}
else if(req.query.title){
    filters.title = req.query.title
}
```

We then check if the *rated* query string exists, then add to the *filters* object. We do the same for *title*.

```
const { moviesList, totalNumMovies } = await MoviesDAO.getMovies({
    filters,
    page,
    moviesPerPage
})
```

We next call *getMovies* in *MoviesDAO* that we have just implemented. Remember that *getMovies* will return *moviesList* and *totalNumMovies*.

```
let response ={
    movies: moviesList,
    page: page,
    filters: filters,
    entries_per_page: moviesPerPage,
    total_results: totalNumMovies,
}
res.json(response)
```

We then send a JSON response with the above response object to whoever calls this URL.

Applying the Controller to our Route

Having completed the controller, let's now apply it to our route. Go to *movies.route.js* and add:

```
import express from 'express'
import MoviesController from './movies.controller.js'

const router = express.Router()

router.route('/').get(MoviesController.apiGetMovies)
```

```
export default router
```

So each time there is a request for URL '/', i.e. *localhost:5000/api/v1/movies/*, we call ***MoviesController.apiGetMovies.***

Let's test our backend API in the next chapter.

CHAPTER 9: TESTING OUR BACKEND API

Now, let's test if our Node backend server can access the database. Go to the browser and type in the URL http://localhost:5000/api/v1/movies and it should send back movie results (fig. 1).

```
{
  "movies": [
    {
      "_id": "573a1390f29313caabcd4135",
      "plot": "Three men hammer on an anvil and pass a bottle of beer around.",
      "genres": [
        "Short"
      ],
      "runtime": 1,
      "cast": [
        "Charles Kayser",
        "John Ott"
      ],
      "num_mflix_comments": 1,
      "title": "Blacksmith Scene",
      "fullplot": "A stationary camera looks at a large anvil with a blacksmith bel
      draws a heated metal rod from the fire, places it on the anvil, and all thre
      metal goes back in the fire. One smith pulls out a bottle of beer, and they
      the hammering resumes.",
      "countries": [
        "USA"
      ],
      "released": "1893-05-09T00:00:00.000Z",
      "directors": [
        "William K.L. Dickson"
      ],
      "rated": "UNRATED",
      "awards": {
        "wins": 1,
        "nominations": 0,
        "text": "1 win."
      },
```

Figure 1

That means our app has successfully queried the database!

Now, we can test the API in our browser, but it is better to test our API with a tool called Insomnia. Go to https://insomnia.rest/ and download the free Insomnia app (fig. 2).

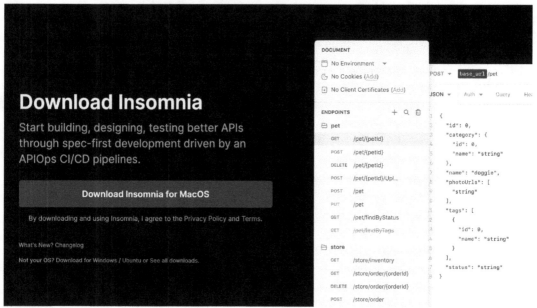

Figure 2

Insomnia helps us test APIs where we can send REST requests to our APIs directly.

Open Insomnia and make a GET request to http://localhost:5000/api/v1/movies (fig. 3).

Figure 3

You should be able to see the retrieved movies on the side (fig. 4).

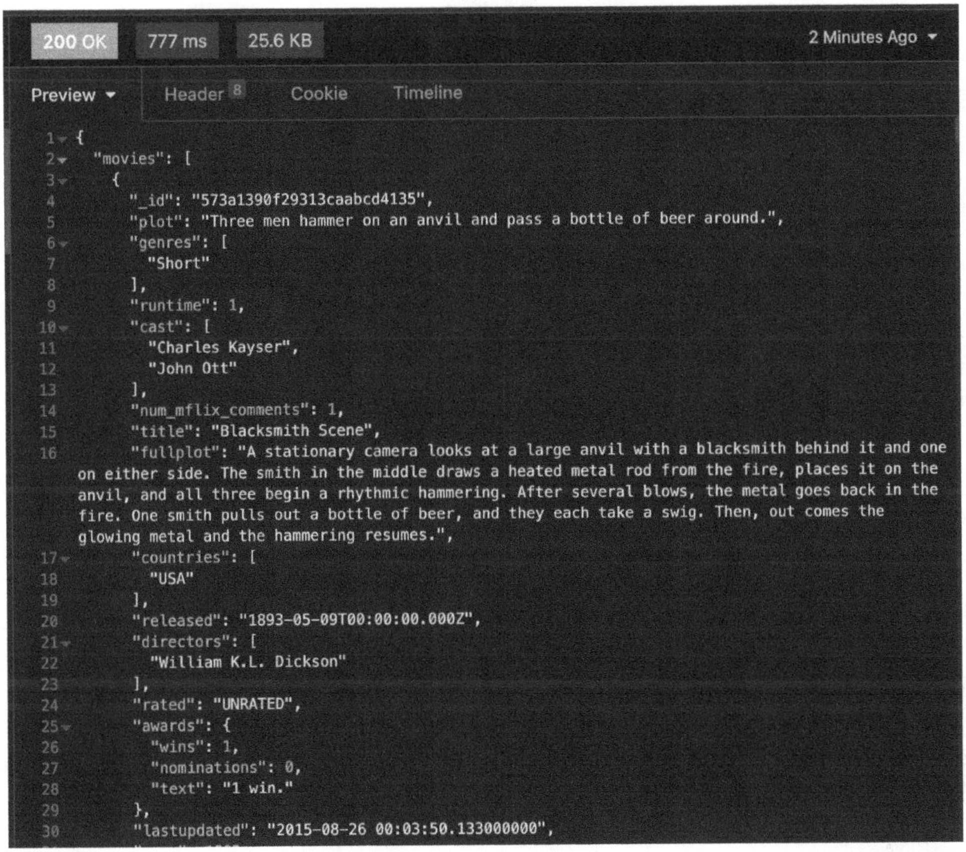

Figure 4

You can see the movie's properties like title, plot etc.

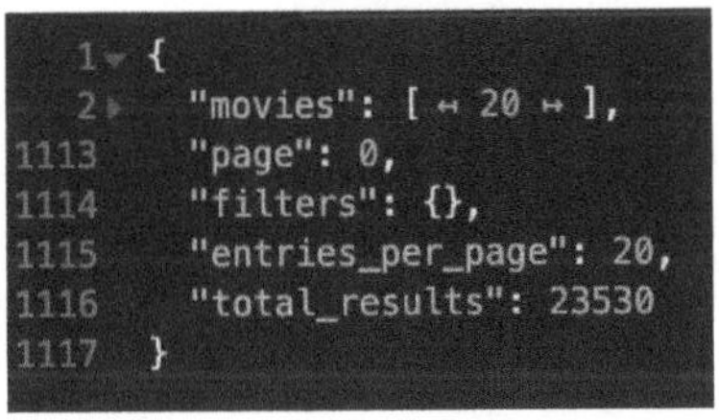

Figure 5

If you collapse the *movies* array, you can see the *page*, *filters* object, *entries_per_page* and *total_results* property in the response as well (fig. 5). This is because back in *movies.controller.js*, we have defined the response in *getMovies* as:

```
...
    let response ={
        movies: moviesList,
        page: page,
        filters: filters,
        entries_per_page: moviesPerPage,
        total_results: totalNumMovies,
    }
    res.json(response)
```

The *page*, *entries_per_page* and *total_results* properties will come in useful later when we implement pagination.

Testing the Filters

Next, let's test the URL with some filters. To apply filters, we add them to the URL query string. For e.g. to filter for movies with rating 'G', we send the following URL in a GET request: http://localhost:5000/api/v1/movies?rated=G and make the request.

You will retrieve movies *rated* 'G'. And at the bottom, we also have the *filters* object, *entries_per_page: 20*, and *total_results: 407* (fig. 6).

```
  1 ▾ {
  2 ▸     "movies": [ ↔ 20 ↔ ],
1349       "page": 0,
1350 ▾     "filters": {
1351         "rated": "G"
1352       },
1353       "entries_per_page": 20,
1354       "total_results": 477
1355     }
```

Figure 6

To filter for page 2, send a GET request to:

http://localhost:5000/api/v1/movies?rated=G&page=2

Search by *title* won't yet work as we have not yet set up the *title* index in MongoDB Atlas. To do so, go to MongoDB Atlas, and in the *sample_mflix* database, *movies* collection, go to 'Indexes' (fig. 7):

Figure 7

Select 'Create Index' and under 'Fields', enter:
```
{
   "title": "text",
}
```

```
COLLECTION
sample_mflix.movies

FIELDS
   1 ▾ {
 i 2      "title": "text",
   3 }
```

Figure 8

Select 'Confirm' and it will create our index to support text search queries on string content. So if you send a request:

*http://localhost:5000/api/v1/movies?title=**Seven***

It will return movie results with *Seven* in its title.

CHAPTER 10: LEAVING MOVIE REVIEWS

Besides searching movies, users can leave reviews for them. So let's create the routes to *post*, *put* and *delete* reviews. *post* is for creating a review, *put* is for editing a review, and *delete* for deleting reviews. In the route file *movies.route.js*, add the routes as shown in **bold**:

```
import express from 'express'
import MoviesController from './movies.controller.js'
import ReviewsController from './reviews.controller.js'

const router = express.Router()

router.route('/').get(MoviesController.apiGetMovies)

router
    .route("/review")
    .post(ReviewsController.apiPostReview)
    .put(ReviewsController.apiUpdateReview)
    .delete(ReviewsController.apiDeleteReview)

export default router
```

Code Explanation

We import the *ReviewsController* which we will create later.

We then add a route '/review' which handles *post*, *put* and *delete* http requests all within this one route call. That is to say, if the '/review' route receives a *post* http request to add a review, we call *apiPostReview*. If '/review' receives a *put* http request to edit a review, call *apiUpdateReview*. And finally, if '/review' receives a *delete* http request to delete a review, call *apiDeleteReview*.

ReviewsController

Next, let's create *reviews.controller.js* with the following code:

```
import ReviewsDAO from '../dao/reviewsDAO.js'
```

```
export default class ReviewsController{
    static async apiPostReview(req,res,next){
        try{
            const movieId = req.body.movie_id
            const review = req.body.review
            const userInfo = {
                name: req.body.name,
                _id: req.body.user_id
            }

            const date = new Date()

            const ReviewResponse = await ReviewsDAO.addReview(
                movieId,
                userInfo,
                review,
                date
            )
            res.json({ status: "success "})
        }catch(e){
            res.status(500).json({ error: e.message})
        }
    }
}
```

Code Explanation

```
import ReviewsDAO from '../dao/reviewsDAO.js'
```

We first import *ReviewsDAO* which we will create later. We then have the *apiPostReview* method:

```
            const movieId = req.body.movie_id
            const review = req.body.review
            const userInfo = {
                name: req.body.name,
                _id: req.body.user_id
            }
```

We get information from the request's *body* parameter. Previously in *MoviesController*, we got information from the request's query parameter as we extracted data from the URL e.g. *req.query.title*. This time, we retrieve the data from the body of the request. In the React frontend of the app (which we will implement later), we call this endpoint with something like:

```
axios.post("https://localhost:5000/api/v1/movies/review", data)
```

The *data* object generated in the frontend will look something like:

```
{
    review: "great movie",
    name: "john",
    user_id: "123",
    movie_id: "573a1390f29313caabcd6223"
}
```

data will be passed in as the request's body. Thus, to retrieve each of the field values, we use *req.body.movie_id, req.body.review* etc.

```
const ReviewResponse = await ReviewsDAO.addReview(
    movieId,
    userInfo,
    review,
    date
)
```

We send the information to *ReviewsDAO.addReview* which we will create later.

```
...
    res.json({ status: "success "})
}catch(e){
    res.status(500).json({ error: e.message})
}
```

Finally, we return 'success' if the post works and an error if it didn't.

ReviewsController *apiUpdateView*

We next create the *apiUpdateReview* method which is quite similar to the *apiPostReview* method.

```
    static async apiUpdateReview(req,res,next){
        try{
            const reviewId = req.body.review_id
            const review = req.body.review

            const date = new Date()

            const ReviewResponse = await ReviewsDAO.updateReview(
                reviewId,
                req.body.user_id,
                review,
                date
            )

            var { error } = ReviewResponse
            if(error){
                res.status.json({error})
            }

            if(ReviewResponse.modifiedCount === 0){
             throw new Error ("unable to update review. User may not be
original poster")
            }
            res.json({ status: "success "})
        }catch(e){
            res.status(500).json({ error: e.message})
        }
    }
}
```

Code Explanation

Like *apiPostReview*, *apiUpdateReview* will be called by the frontend with a request like the below:

```
axios.put("https://localhost:5000/api/v1/movies/review", data)
```

We extract the *movieId* and *review* text similar to what we have done in posting a review.

```
        const ReviewResponse = await ReviewsDAO.updateReview(
            reviewId,
            req.body.user_id,
```

```
            review,
            date
        )
```

We then call *ReviewsDAO.updateReview* and pass in *user_id* to ensure that the user who is updating the view is the one who has created it.

```
        if(ReviewResponse.modifiedCount === 0){
            throw new Error ("unable to update review. user may not be
original poster")
        }
```

updateReview returns a document *ReviewResponse* which contains the property *modifiedCount*. *modifiedCount* contains the number of modified documents. We check *modifiedCount* to ensure that it is not zero. If it is, it means the review has not been updated and we throw an error.

ReviewsController *apiDeleteView*

We lastly have *apiDeleteReview*:

```
    static async apiDeleteReview(req,res,next){
        try{
            const reviewId = req.body.review_id
            const userId = req.body.user_id
            const ReviewResponse = await ReviewsDAO.deleteReview(
                reviewId,
                userId,
            )

            res.json({ status: "success "})
        }catch(e){
            res.status(500).json({ error: e.message})
        }
    }
```

Like *apiPostReview* and *apiUpdateReview*, we extract *reviewId* and *userId*. With *userId*, we ensure that the user deleting the view is the one who has created the view. Now, let's create *ReviewsDAO*.

ReviewsDAO

In *dao* folder, create the file *reviewsDAO.js* with the following code:

```
import mongodb from "mongodb"
const ObjectId = mongodb.ObjectId

let reviews

export default class ReviewsDAO{
    static async injectDB(conn){
        if(reviews){
            return
        }
        try{
            reviews = await
conn.db(process.env.MOVIEREVIEWS_NS).collection('reviews')
        }
        catch(e){
            console.error(`unable to establish connection handle in
reviewDAO: ${e}`)
        }
    }
}
```

Code Explanation

```
import mongodb from "mongodb"
const ObjectId = mongodb.ObjectId
```

We import *mongodb* to get access to *ObjectId*. We need *ObjectId* to convert an id string to a MongoDB Object id later on.

```
        if(reviews){
            return
        }
        try{
            reviews = await
conn.db(process.env.MOVIEREVIEWS_NS).collection('reviews')
```

```
    }
```

For the rest of the code, notice that it is similar to *MoviesDAO*. If *reviews* is not filled, we then access the database *reviews* collection. Note that if the *reviews* collection doesn't yet exist in the database, MongoDB automatically creates it for us.

Initiating ReviewsDAO in index.js

We will also need to initiate *ReviewsDAO* as we did for *MoviesDAO* in *index.js*. In *index.js*, add in the below two lines:

```
import app from './server.js'
import mongodb from "mongodb"
import dotenv from "dotenv"
import MoviesDAO from './dao/moviesDAO.js'
import ReviewsDAO from './dao/reviewsDAO.js'

async function main(){
    ...
    try {
        await client.connect()
        await MoviesDAO.injectDB(client)
        await ReviewsDAO.injectDB(client)

        app.listen(port, () =>{
            console.log('server is running on port:'+port);
        })
    }
    ...
}
main().catch(console.error);
```

ReviewsDAO addReview

In *reviewsDAO.js*, add in the *addReview* method for creating a review:

```
    static async addReview(movieId, user, review, date){
        try{
            const reviewDoc = {
                name: user.name,
```

```
            user_id: user._id,
            date: date,
            review: review,
            movie_id: ObjectId(movieId)
        }
        return await reviews.insertOne(reviewDoc)
    }
    catch(e){
        console.error(`unable to post review: ${e}`)
        return { error: e}
    }
}
```

We first create a *reviewDoc* document object. Note that for the *movie_id*, we have to first convert the *movieId* string to a MongoDB object id. We then insert it into the *reviews* collection with *insertOne*.

ReviewsDAO updateReview

In *reviewsDAO.js*, add in the below *updateReview* method for editing a review:

```
static async updateReview(reviewId, userId, review, date){
    try{
        const updateResponse = await reviews.updateOne(
            {user_id: userId,_id: ObjectId(reviewId)},
            {$set:{review:review, date: date}}
        )
        return updateResponse
    }
    catch(e){
        console.error(`unable to update review: ${e}`)
        return { error: e}
    }
}
```

When calling *reviews.updateOne*, we specify the first argument {user_id: userId,_id: ObjectId(reviewId)} to filter for an existing review created by *userId* and with *reviewId*. If the review exists, we then update it with the second argument which contains the new review text and date.

ReviewsDAO deleteReview

In *reviewsDAO.js*, add in the below *deleteReview* method for deleting a review:

```
static async deleteReview(reviewId, userId){
    try{
        const deleteResponse = await reviews.deleteOne({
          _id: ObjectId(reviewId),
          user_id: userId,
        })
        return deleteResponse
    }
    catch(e){
        console.error(`unable to delete review: ${e}`)
        return { error: e}
    }
}
```

When calling *reviews.deleteOne*, similar to *updateOne*, we specify `ObjectId(reviewId)` to look for an existing review with *reviewId* and created by *userId*. If the review exists, we then delete it.

CHAPTER 11: TESTING THE REVIEWS API

To test the reviews API, first get an existing movie id. You can just send a *get* request to
http://localhost:5000/api/v1/movies to retrieve all movies and then pick any movie id.

Next, make a *post* request to: *localhost:5000/api/v1/movies/review* and provide a review body something like:

```
{
  "movie_id": "573a1390f29313caabcd4135",
  "review": "great movie",
  "user_id": "1234",
  "name": "john"
}
```

Figure 1

*Note: Make sure that *movie_id* is in a valid *ObjectID* format. Else, MongoDB will not accept it and will throw an error something like:

"**Error: Argument passed in must be a single String of 12 bytes or a string of 24 hex characters**"

Click 'Send' and you should get a *status: success* response. And if you go to MongoDB Atlas, your newly posted review should be in the *reviews* collection.

Testing Edit

Now let's see if we can edit a review. We will need the *review_id* of an existing review. With the *review_id*, send a *put* request in Insomnia to *localhost:5000/api/v1/movies/review* with a JSON object like:

```
{
  "review_id": "60987656387806c22051bb67",
  "review": "bad movie",
  "user_id": "1234",
  "name": "john"
}
```

And if you go to MongoDB Atlas (you might need to refresh it), the review should be edited.

Testing Delete

Now, let's test the *delete* review endpoint. Send a *delete* request to *localhost:5000/api/v1/movies/review* with a JSON object like:

```
{
  "review_id": "609879ea2c7565c289746500",
  "user_id": "1234"
}
```

And if you go to MongoDB Atlas and select refresh, the review will no longer exist.

So, we have tested our add, edit and delete review API endpoints!

CHAPTER 12: ROUTE TO GET A SINGLE MOVIE AND ITS RATINGS

We are getting close to completing the back end. We just need to add two more routes, a route to get a specific movie (with its reviews) and a route to get all ratings. In the *movies.route.js* route file, add the two routes as shown:

```
...
router.route('/').get(MoviesController.apiGetMovies)
router.route("/id/:id").get(MoviesController.apiGetMovieById)
router.route("/ratings").get(MoviesController.apiGetRatings)
...
```

Code Explanation

```
router.route("/id/:id").get(MoviesController.apiGetMovieById)
```

This route retrieves a specific movie and all reviews associated for that movie.

```
router.route("/ratings").get(MoviesController.apiGetRating)
```

This route returns us a list of movie ratings (e.g. 'G', 'PG', 'R') so that a user can select the ratings from a dropdown menu in the front end.

movies.controller.js

Next, let's implement the *apiGetMovieById* and *apiGetRatings* methods in *MoviesController*. Add in the following two methods into *movies.controller.js*:

```
import MoviesDAO from '../dao/moviesDAO.js'

export default class MoviesController{
    ...
    static async apiGetMovieById(req,res, next){
        try{
            let id = req.params.id || {}
            let movie = await MoviesDAO.getMovieById(id)
```

```
        if(!movie){
            res.status(404).json({ error: "not found"})
            return
        }
        res.json(movie)
    }
    catch(e){
        console.log(`api, ${e}`)
        res.status(500).json({error: e})
    }
}


static async apiGetRatings(req,res,next){
    try{
        let propertyTypes = await MoviesDAO.getRatings()
        res.json(propertyTypes)
    }
    catch(e){
        console.log(`api,${e}`)
        res.status(500).json({error: e})
    }
}
}
```

Code Explanation

```
        let id = req.params.id || {}
```

We first look for an *id* parameter which is the value after the '/' in a URL. E.g. *localhost:5000/api/v1/movies/id/12345*

Note the difference between a request query and parameter. In a query, there is a '?' after the URL followed by a key-value e.g. /api/v1/movies?title=dragon
In a parameter, it's the value after '/'.

```
        let movie = await MoviesDAO.getMovieById(id)
        if(!movie){
            res.status(404).json({ error: "not found"})
            return
        }
        res.json(movie)
```

We then call *MoviesDAO.getMovieById* which we will create later. The method returns us the specific movie in a JSON response. If there is no movie, we return an error.

The *apiGetRatings* is more straightforward. We do not have to feed in any parameters, but simply call *MoviesDAO.apiGetRatings*.

Implementing *getMovieById* and *getRatings* in *MoviesDAO*

We will first implement *getRatings* in *moviesDAO.js* as it is more straightforward. Add the below method into *moviesDAO*:

```
static async getRatings(){
    let ratings = []
    try{
        ratings = await movies.distinct("rated")
        return ratings
    }
    catch(e){
        console.error(`unable to get ratings, $(e)`)
        return ratings
    }
}
```

We use *movies.distinct* to get all the distinct *rated* values from the *movies* collection. We then assign the results to the *ratings* array.

getMovieById

Next, let's implement *getMovieById* which can be a little complicated because other than getting the specific movie from the *movies* collection, we will also be getting its related reviews from the *reviews* collection.

Add the below method and the import statement in **bold** into *moviesDAO*:

```
import mongodb from "mongodb"
const ObjectId = mongodb.ObjectID

let movies
```

```
export default class MoviesDAO{
    ...
    static async getMovieById(id){
        try{
            return await movies.aggregate([
                {
                    $match: {
                        _id: new ObjectId(id),
                    }
                }   ,
                { $lookup:
                    {
                        from: 'reviews',
                        localField: '_id',
                        foreignField: 'movie_id',
                        as: 'reviews',
                    }
                }
            ]).next()
        }
        catch(e){
            console.error(`something went wrong in getMovieById: ${e}`)
            throw e
        }
    }
    ...
}
```

Code Explanation

We use *aggregate* to provide a sequence of data aggregation operations. In our case, the first operation is *$match*, where we look for the movie document that matches the specified id.

Next, we use the *$lookup* operator to perform an equality join using the *_id* field from the *movie* document with the *movie_id* field from *reviews* collection.

The *$lookup* stage has the following syntax:

```
{
    $lookup:
      {
        from: <collection to join>,
        localField: <field from the input document>,
        foreignField: <field from the documents of the "from" collection>,
        as: <output array field>
      }
}
```

This finds all the reviews with the specific movie id and returns the specific movie together with the reviews in an array.

$lookup is just one component of the MongoDB aggregation framework. MongoDB aggregations are very powerful but we will just touch a small part of this now.

Testing our App

Now, let's test the two routes we have added into *movies.route.js*:

```
router.route("/id/:id").get(MoviesController.apiGetMovieById)
router.route("/ratings").get(MoviesController.apiGetRatings)
```

Let's first test the */ratings* route. Send a *GET* request to: *localhost:5000/api/v1/movies/ratings/*. You should get all the ratings returned:

```
[
    "AO",
    "APPROVED",
    "Approved",
    "G",
    "GP",
    "M",
    "NC-17",
    "NOT RATED",
    "Not Rated",
    "OPEN",
    "PASSED",
    "PG",
    "PG-13",
```

```
  "R",
  "TV-14",
  "TV-G",
  "TV-MA",
  "TV-PG",
  "TV-Y7",
  "UNRATED",
  "X"
]
```

We will later use this to populate the dropdown menu.

Testing our app – Get Specific Movie

Next, let's test the */id/:id* route. Send a GET request to:

`localhost:5000/api/v1/movies/id/573a1390f29313caabcd6223`
(fill in your own movie id)

and you should get the specific movie data and the *reviews* array in the response too.

```
{
  "_id": "573a1390f29313caabcd6223",
  "plot": "..",
  "genres": [
    "Comedy",
    "Drama",
    "Family"
  ],
  "runtime": 65,
  "cast": [
    "Mary Pickford",
    "Madlaine Traverse",
    "Charles Wellesley",
    "Gladys Fairbanks"
  ],
  "title": "The Poor Little Rich Girl",
       ...
  "reviews": [
    {
      "_id": "6098bdd132398dc6576a89a8",
```

```
      "name": "jason",
      "user_id": "1234",
      "date": "2021-05-10T05:00:01.675Z",
      "review": "nice!",
      "movie_id": "573a1390f29313caabcd6223"
    },
    {
      "_id": "6098bddf32398dc6576a89a9",
      "name": "john",
      "user_id": "1236",
      "date": "2021-05-10T05:00:15.380Z",
      "review": "bad!",
      "movie_id": "573a1390f29313caabcd6223"
    }
  ]
}
```

If the *reviews* array is empty, create some reviews for the movie first by sending POST requests to *localhost:5000/api/v1/movies/review/* and JSON objects to add the reviews e.g.

```
{
  "movie_id":"573a1390f29313caabcd6223",
  "review":"nice!",
  "user_id":"1234",
  "name":"jason",
}

{
  "movie_id":"573a1390f29313caabcd6223",
  "review":"bad!",
  "user_id":"1236",
  "name":"john"
}
```

Send the GET request to get the specific movie again and you should get *reviews* populated in the response.

And that completes our backend implemented with Node and Express. All our routes work. So let's create our frontend and then connect it to our backend.

REACT FRONTEND

CHAPTER 13: INTRODUCTION TO REACT

For those who have some experience with React, this section will be familiar to you. But even if you are new to React, you should still be able to follow along. If you are interested in digging into React details, you can check out my React book.

Before we go on further, let's explain briefly what is React. React is a framework released by Facebook for creating user interfaces with components. For example, if we want to build a storefront module like what we see on Amazon, we can divide it into three components. The search bar component, sidebar component and products component (fig. 1).

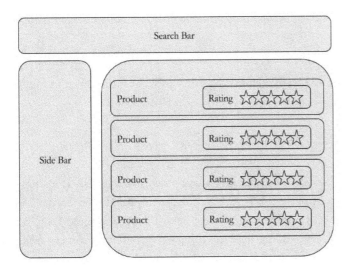

Figure 1

Components can also contain other components. For example, in *products* component where we display a list of products, we do so using multiple *product* components. Also, in each *product* component, we can have a *rating* component.

The benefit of such an architecture helps us to break up a large application into smaller manageable components. Plus, we can reuse components within the application or even in a different application. For example, we can re-use the rating component in a different application.

A React component contains a JSX template that ultimately outputs HTML elements. It has its own data and logic to control the JSX template. When the values of its data changes, React will update the concerned UI component.

Below is an example of a component that displays a simple string 'Products'.

```
import React from 'react';

function Products() {
    return (
      <div>
        <h2>
            Products
        </h2>
      </div>
    );
}


export default Products;
```

The function returns a React element in JSX syntax which determines what is displayed in the UI. JSX is a syntax extension to Javascript. JSX converts to HTML when processed.

Creating the React Project folder

We will create our initial React project by using 'create-react-app'. *'create-react-app'* (CRA) is the best way to start building a new React single page application. It sets up our development environment so that we can use the latest Javascript features and optimization for our app. It is a Command Line Interface tool that makes creating a new React project, adding files and other on-going development tasks like testing, bundling and deployment easier. It uses build tools like Babel and Webpack under the hood and provides a pleasant developer experience for us that we don't have to do any manual configurations for it.

First, let's go to our *movie-reviews* directory and in it, we will use *create-react-app* to create our React app. We can actually create a React app without installing CRA by running:

```
npx create-react-app <project name>
```

In our case, our project will be called *frontend*. So run:

```
npx create-react-app frontend
```

Note: The reason we are using *npx* is because *create-react-app* is a package expected to be run only once in our project. So it is more convenient to run it only once rather than downloading it on to our machine and then use it.

create-react-app will create a directory 'frontend' containing the default React project template with all the dependencies installed. When the folder is created, navigate to it by typing in the Terminal:

```
cd frontend
```

and then run:

```
npm start
```

Your browser will then show a moving React icon (fig. 1) which shows that React is loaded successfully.

Figure 1

Project File Review

Now let's look at the project files that have been created for us. When you open the *movie-reviews/frontend* project folder in VScode editor, you will find a couple of files (fig. 2).

fig. 2

We will not go through all the files as our focus is to get started with our React app quickly, but we will briefly go through some of the more important files and folders.

Our app lives in the *src* folder. All React components, CSS styles, images (e.g. logo.svg) and anything else our app needs go here. Any other files outside of this folder are meant to support building your app (the app folder is where we will work 99% of the time!). In the course of this book, you will come to appreciate the uses for the rest of the library files and folders.

In the *src* folder, we have *index.js* which is the main entry point for our app. In *index.js*, we render the *App* React element into the root DOM node. Applications built with just React usually have a single root DOM node.

index.js

```
import React from 'react';
import ReactDOM from 'react-dom';
import './index.css';
import App from './App';
import * as serviceWorker from './serviceWorker';

ReactDOM.render(
  <React.StrictMode>
```

```
  <App />
</React.StrictMode>,
  document.getElementById('root')
);
```

```
serviceWorker.unregister();
```

In *index.js*, we import both React and ReactDOM which we need to work with React in the browser. React is the library for creating views. ReactDOM is the library used to render the UI in the browser. The two libraries were split into two packages for version 0.14 and the purpose for splitting is to allow for components to be shared between the web version of React and React Native, thus supporting rendering for a variety of platforms.

index.js imports *index.css*, App component and *serviceWorker* with the following lines.

```
import './index.css';
import App from './App';
import * as serviceWorker from './serviceWorker';
```

It then renders App with:

```
ReactDOM.render(
  <React.StrictMode>
    <App />
  </React.StrictMode>,
  document.getElementById('root')
);
```

The last line `serviceWorker.unregister()` has comments:

```
// If you want your app to work offline and load faster, you can change
// unregister() to register() below. Note this comes with some pitfalls.
// Learn more about service workers: https://bit.ly/CRA-PWA
```

serviceWorker.register() is meant to create progressive web apps (PWA) catered more for mobile React Native apps to work offline. This however is out of the scope of this book and we can safely leave the code as `serviceWorker.unregister()` for now.

App.js is the main React code that we display on the page.

App.js

```
import logo from './logo.svg';
import './App.css';

function App() {
  return (
    <div className="App">
      <header className="App-header">
        <img src={logo} className="App-logo" alt="logo" />
        <p>
          Edit <code>src/App.js</code> and save to reload.
        </p>
        <a
          className="App-link"
          href="https://reactjs.org"
          target="_blank"
          rel="noopener noreferrer"
        >
          Learn React
        </a>
      </header>
    </div>
  );
}

export default App;
```

Note: any element that has an HTML class attribute is using *className* for that property instead of *class*. Since *class* is a reserved word in Javascript, we have to use *className* to define the class attribute of an HTML element.

In the above, we have a functional-based component called *App*. Every React application has at least one component: the root component, named *App* in *App.js*. The App component controls the view through the JSX template it returns:

```
  return (
      <div className="App">
          ...
      </div>
  );
```

A component has to return a **single** React element. In our case, *App* returns a single *<div />*. The element can be a representation of a native DOM component, such as *<div />*, or another composite component that you've defined yourself.

Components can either be *functional* based or *class* based. We will talk more on this later, but as a starter, what we have in *App* is a functional-based component as seen from its header *function App()*.

Add React bootstrap framework:

We will use React *bootstrap* to make our UI look more professional. React Bootstrap (https://react-bootstrap.github.io) is a library of reusable frontend components that contain JSX based templates to help build user interface components (like forms, buttons, icons) for web applications.

To install React bootstrap, in the Terminal, run:

```
npm install react-bootstrap bootstrap
```

React-Router-DOM

We will next install *react-router-dom* to route different URLs to different pages in our React app. The *React Router* library interprets a browser URL as an instruction to navigate to various components.

We can bind the router to links on a page and it will navigate to the appropriate application view when the user clicks a link.

Install the *react-router-dom* library by executing the below in the Terminal:

```
npm install --save react-router-dom
```

Test our App

Now, let's make sure that everything is working so far. Fill in *App.js* with the below code.

```
import React from 'react'
import { Switch, Route, Link } from "react-router-dom"
import "bootstrap/dist/css/bootstrap.min.css"

function App() {
  return (
```

```
    <div className="App">
      Hello World
    </div>
  );
}

export default App;
```

Code Explanation

Switch, Route and *Link* are imported from the 'react-router-dom' library which help us create different URL routes to different components.
Bootstrap as mentioned earlier provides styling to our whole app.
And in the *return* method, we have a single and simple component with the message 'Hello World'.

Test Run

To test run our app, go to the *frontend* directory in the Terminal and run:

```
npm start
```

It will then open up *localhost:3000* in your browser and print out the message 'Hello World' (fig. 3).

Hello World

Figure 3

So our React app's running well. In the next chapter, we will create a navigation header bar in our app.

CHAPTER 14: CREATE NAVIGATION HEADER BAR

Let's add a navigation header bar which allows a user to select different routes to access different components in the main part of the page. We will start by creating some simple components and our router will load the different components depending on the URL route a user selects.

Let's first create a *components* folder in *src* (fig. 1).

Figure 1

In the *components* folder, we will create four new component files:

movies-list.js – a component to list movies
*movie.j*s – a component to list a single movie
add-review.js – component to add a review
login.js – login component

Let's first have a simple boilerplate code for each component:

movies-list.js

```
import React from 'react'

function MoviesList() {
```

```
  return (
    <div className="App">
      Movies List
    </div>
  );
}

export default MoviesList;
```

movie.js

```
import React from 'react'

function Movie() {
  return (
    <div className="App">
      Movie
    </div>
  );
}

export default Movie;
```

add-review.js

```
import React from 'react'

function AddReview() {
  return (
    <div className="App">
      Add Review
    </div>
  );
}

export default AddReview;
```

login.js

```
import React from 'react'

function Login() {
```

```
  return (
    <div className="App">
      Login
    </div>
  );
}

export default Login;
```

We will later revisit the above components and implement them in greater detail.

Next in *App.js*, import the newly created components:

```
import React from 'react'
import { Switch, Route, Link } from "react-router-dom"
import "bootstrap/dist/css/bootstrap.min.css"

import AddReview from "./components/add-review"
import MoviesList from "./components/movies-list"
import Movie from "./components/movie"
import Login from "./components/login"

function App() {
  return (
    <div className="App">
      Hello World
    </div>
  );
}
export default App;
```

React-Bootstrap Navbar Component

Next, we will grab a navbar component from React-Bootstrap (https://react-bootstrap.github.io/components/navbar/ fig. 2)

Figure 2

Paste the markup into *App.js* by adding the following codes:

```
...
import Nav from 'react-bootstrap/Nav'
import Navbar from 'react-bootstrap/Navbar'
...
function App() {
  return (
    <div className="App">
      <Navbar bg="light" expand="lg">
        <Navbar.Brand href="#home">React-Bootstrap</Navbar.Brand>
        <Navbar.Toggle aria-controls="basic-navbar-nav" />
        <Navbar.Collapse id="basic-navbar-nav">
          <Nav className="mr-auto">
            <Nav.Link href="#home">Home</Nav.Link>
            <Nav.Link href="#link">Link</Nav.Link>
          </Nav>
        </Navbar.Collapse>
      </Navbar>
    </div>
  );
}


export default App;
```

Bootstrap has different components that you can use. To use a component, go to the Bootstrap documentation (*https://react-bootstrap.github.io/*), copy the component's markup and update it for your own purposes.

Note that I have dropped the *NavDropdown* and *Search* form elements from the *Navbar* for simplicity. So we just have a basic bootstrap navbar. If you run the app now, it should give you something like in figure 3:

Figure 3

In the current navbar, we have three links. The first is 'React-bootstrap' which is like the brand of the website. Sometimes, this would be a logo, image, or just some text. We will leave it as a text.

The other two are links to 'Home' and 'Link'. We will change 'Home' to 'Movies' and link it to '/movies'. We will remove 'Link' and replace it with 'Login' or 'Logout' depending on the user's login state.

So make the following changes in **bold**:

```
<Navbar bg="light" expand="lg">
  <Navbar.Brand>Movie Reviews</Navbar.Brand>
  <Navbar.Toggle aria-controls="basic-navbar-nav" />
  <Navbar.Collapse id="basic-navbar-nav">
    <Nav className="mr-auto">
      <Nav.Link>
        <Link to={"/movies"}>Movies</Link>
      </Nav.Link>
      <Nav.Link>
        { user ? (
          <a>Logout User</a>
        ) : (
          <Link to={"/login"}>Login</Link>
        )}
      </Nav.Link>
    </Nav>
  </Navbar.Collapse>
</Navbar>
```

Code Explanation

```
<Link to={"/movies"}>Movies</Link>
```

We use the *Link* component imported from *react-router-dom*. *Link* allows us to route to a different component. So when a user clicks on 'Movies', it will route to the *movies* component. The actual route definition will be implemented and explained in the next chapter.

```
{ user ? (
  <a>Logout User</a>
) : (
  <Link to={"/login"}>Login</Link>
)}
```

For the second link, if the user is not logged in, we will show 'Login' which links to the login component. If the user is logged in, it will show 'Logout User' which will link to the logout component.

How do we achieve this conditional rendering? In React, we can use curly braces '{}' to put in code. The code is a ternary statement where if its true, execute the section after the '?'. If false, execute the section after the colon ':'. For e.g. if you hardcode *user* to true, it will always show 'Logout User': e.g.

```
{ user true ? (
  <a>Logout User</a>
) : (
  <Link to={"/login"}>Login</Link>
)}
```

Let's test our app now to see how it looks like. But before that, we need to enclose our *Link*s in a *BrowserRouter*. To do so, in *index.js*, add:

```
import React from 'react';
import ReactDOM from 'react-dom';
import App from './App';
import {BrowserRouter} from 'react-router-dom';

ReactDOM.render(
  <BrowserRouter>
    <App />
  </BrowserRouter>,
  document.getElementById('root')
);
```

And if you run your app, it should look like figure 4:

Figure 4

If you change *user* to *false*:

```
{ user false ? (
  <a>Logout User</a>
) : (
```

84

```
          <Link to={"/login"}>Login</Link>
      )}
```

it will show the *Login* link (fig. 5).

Movie Reviews   Movies Login

Figure 5

We should of course not leave it hard-coded as true or false. Make sure you change it back to *user*:

```
{ user ? (
  <a>Logout User</a>
) : (
  <Link to={"/login"}>Login</Link>
)}
```

Login Logout

In this section, we will replace the hardcoding to reflect the actual login state of a user and also implement a preliminary login-logout function. Let's first declare a *user* state variable using React hooks by adding the below in *App.js*:

```
...
function App() {
  const [user, setUser] = React.useState(null)

  async function login(user = null){// default user to null
    setUser(user)
  }

  async function logout(){
    setUser(null)
  }

  return (
    <div className="App">
      ...
                <Nav.Link>
```

```
            { user ? (
              <a onClick={logout}>Logout User</a>
            ) : (
              <Link to={"/login"}>Login</Link>
            )}
          </Nav.Link>
    ...
    </div>
  );
}
```

Code Explanation

```
const [user, setUser] = React.useState(null)
```

React.useState is a 'hook' that lets us add some local state to functional components. *useState* declares a 'state variable'. React preserves this state between re-renders of the component. In our case, our state consists of a *user* variable to represent either a logged in or logged out state. When we pass null to *useState*, i.e. *useState(null)*, we specify *null* to be the initial value for *user*.

useState returns an array with two values: the current state value and a function that lets you update it. In our case, we assign the current state user value to *user*, and the function to update it to *setUser*.

```
async function login(user = null){// default user to null
  setUser(user)
}

async function logout(){
  setUser(null)
}
```

With *login*, we set the *user* state. The *login* function will be called from the Login component which we will implement and re-visit later.

```
            { user ? (
              <a onClick={logout}>Logout User</a>
            ) : (
              <Link to={"/login"}>Login</Link>
            )}
```

logout() simply sets *user* to null.

For our app, we won't be implementing a full login system as it is outside the scope of this book. But we have a preliminary login where you can update it with a full-fledged login using Google sign-in, Firebase, OAuth or other authentication providers.

CHAPTER 15: DEFINING OUR ROUTES

After the navbar section in *App.js*, add the *route* section by adding the below codes in **bold**:

```
<div className="App">
  <Navbar bg="light" expand="lg">
    ...
  </Navbar>

  <Switch>
    <Route exact path={["/", "/movies"]} component={MoviesList}>
    </Route>
    <Route path="/movies/:id/review" render={(props)=>
      <AddReview {...props} user={user} />
    }>
    </Route>
    <Route path="/movies/:id/" render={(props)=>
      <Movie {...props} user={user} />
    }>
    </Route>
    <Route path="/login" render={(props)=>
      <Login {...props} login={login} />
    }>
    </Route>
  </Switch>
</div>
```

Code Explanation

We use a *Switch* component to switch between different routes. The *Switch* component renders the first route that matches.

```
<Route exact path={["/", "/movies"]} component={MoviesList}>
</Route>
```

We first have the exact path route. If the path is "/" or "/movies", show the *MoviesList* component.

```
<Route path="/movies/:id/review" render={(props)=>
  <AddReview {...props} user={user} />
}>
```

89

We then have the route for "**/movies/:id/review**". Note that we use *render* instead of *component* because *render* allows us to pass in *props* into a component rendered by React Router. In this case, we are passing *user* (the logged-in user information) as *props* to the *AddReview* component. We can pass data into a component by passing in a object called *props*.

We will see later how props work when we implement the *AddReview* component.

We then next have the routes for a specific movie "**/movies/:id/**" and "**/login**" to render the *Movie* and *Login* component respectively.

```
<Route path="/login" render={(props)=>
  <Login {...props} login={login} />
}>
```

Note that the login route passes in the *login* function as a prop:

```
async function login(user = null){// default user to null
  setUser(user)
}
```

This allows the *login* function to be called from the *Login* component and thus populate the *user* state variable as we will see later.

Testing our Routes

If you run your React frontend now and click on the different links in the navbar, you will see the different components being rendered (fig. 1).

Movie Reviews   Movies   Login

Movies List

Figure 1

CHAPTER 16: MOVIEDATASERVICE: CONNECTING TO THE BACKEND

To retrieve the list of movies from the database, we will need to connect to our backend server. We will create a *service* class for that. A service is a class with a well-defined specific function your app needs. In our case, our service is responsible for talking to the backend to get and save data. Service classes provide their functionality to be consumed by components. We will cover components in the next chapter.

Under *src*, create a new folder called *services*. In *services*, create a new file *movies.js* with the following code:

```javascript
import axios from "axios";

class MovieDataService{

  getAll(page = 0){
    return axios.get(`http://localhost:5000/api/v1/movies?page=${page}`)
  }

  get(id){
    return axios.get(`http://localhost:5000/api/v1/movies/id/${id}`)
  }

  find(query, by = "title", page = 0){
    return axios.get(
     `http://localhost:5000/api/v1/movies?${by}=${query}&page=${page}`
    )
  }

  createReview(data){
    return axios.post("http://localhost:5000/api/v1/movies/review", data)
  }
  updateReview(data){
    return axios.put("http://localhost:5000/api/v1/movies/review", data)
  }
  deleteReview(id, userId){
    return axios.delete(
      "http://localhost:5000/api/v1/movies/review",
      {data:{review_id: id, user_id: userId}}
    )
  }
```

91

```
  getRatings(){
    return axios.get("http://localhost:5000/api/v1/movies/ratings")
  }
}
export default new MovieDataService()
```

Code Explanation

```
import axios from "axios"
```

We use a library called *axios* for sending *get*, *post*, *put* and *delete* request. Let's first install *axios* by running in Terminal:

```
npm install axios
```

The class *MovieDataService* contains functions which make the API calls to the backend endpoints we have implemented and return the results.

```
  getAll(page = 0){
    return axios.get(`http://localhost:5000/api/v1/movies?page=${page}`)
  }
```

getAll returns all the movies for a particular page (default page request is 0). We put the API URL into the *axios.get* method. This endpoint is served by the method *apiGetMovies* in *MoviesController* (refer to chapter 8).

```
  get(id){
    return axios.get(`http://localhost:5000/api/v1/movies/id/${id}`)
  }
```

get(id) gets the specific movie with the supplied id. This endpoint is served by the method *apiGetMovieById* in *MoviesController* (refer to chapter 12).

```
  find(query, by = "title", page = 0){
    return axios.get(
      `http://localhost:5000/api/v1/movies?${by}=${query}&page=${page}`
    )
  }
```

find() connects to the same endpoint as *getAll* except that it has *query* which consists of the user-entered search title, ratings (e.g. 'G') and page number.

The remaining four methods are for creating, updating and deleting a review and to get all ratings. We will later revisit the entire flow from the frontend to the backend after implementing the React frontend.

CHAPTER 17: MOVIESLIST COMPONENT

Let's now implement the *MoviesList* component to consume the functionality in *MovieDataService*. Components are meant to be responsible for mainly rendering views supported by application logic for better user experience. They don't fetch data from the backend but rather delegate such tasks to services.

We will carry on implementing our *MoviesList* component. Fill in the below code into *movies-list.js*:

```
import React, {useState, useEffect } from 'react'
import MovieDataService from "../services/movies"
import { Link } from "react-router-dom"

const MoviesList = props => {

  const [movies, setMovies] = useState([])
  const [searchTitle, setSearchTitle] = useState("")
  const [searchRating, setSearchRating] = useState("")
  const [ratings, setRatings] = useState(["All Ratings"])
}
```

Code Explanation

```
import React, {useState, useEffect } from 'react'
import MovieDataService from "../services/movies"
import { Link } from "react-router-dom"
```

We import *useState* to create a series of state variables. We import *useEffect* (which we will describe later) and also import *MovieDataService* and *Link*.

```
const MoviesList = props => {
  const [movies, setMovies] = useState([])
  const [searchTitle, setSearchTitle] = useState("")
  const [searchRating, setSearchRating] = useState("")
  const [ratings, setRatings] = useState(["All Ratings"])=
}
```

MoviesList is a functional component and receives and uses props. We use the React *useState* hook to create the *movies*, *searchTitle*, *searchRating* and *ratings* state variables. The *searchTitle* and *searchRating* state variables keep track of what a user has entered into the search form fields in the Movies List page.

95

Note that *movies* is default set to an empty array `useState([])`. *ratings* is by default set to an array with a value "All Ratings". This is because when a user first comes to the Movies List search form, the default value for search by ratings is 'All Ratings' i.e. `useState(["All Ratings"])`. *searchTitle* and *searchRating* are default set to an empty string, `useState("")`.

useEffect to retrieveMovies and Ratings

Next, we add the *useEffect* hook and the *retrieveMovies* and *retrieveRatings* methods as shown:

```
...
const MoviesList= props => {

  const [movies, setMovies] = useState([])
  const [searchTitle, setSearchTitle] = useState("")
  const [searchRating, setSearchRating] = useState("")
  const [ratings, setRatings] = useState(["All Ratings"])

  useEffect(() =>{
    retrieveMovies()
    retrieveRatings()
  },[])

  const retrieveMovies = () =>{
    MovieDataService.getAll()
      .then(response =>{
        console.log(response.data)
        setMovies(response.data.movies)
      })
      .catch( e =>{
        console.log(e)
      })
  }

  const retrieveRatings = () =>{
    MovieDataService.getRatings()
      .then(response =>{
        console.log(response.data)
        //start with 'All ratings' if user doesn't specify any ratings
        setRatings(["All Ratings"].concat(response.data))
      })
```

96

```
      .catch( e =>{
        console.log(e)
      })
  }
```

Code Explanation

```
useEffect(() =>{
  retrieveMovies()
  retrieveRatings()
},[])
```

The *useEffect* hook is called after the component renders. So if we want to tell the component to perform some code after rendering, we include it here. In our case, after the component renders, we want to retrieve movies and ratings.

*Note that it is important that we specify an empty array in the second argument of *useEffect*. When we do so, *useEffect* is called only once when the component first renders. Without the second argument, *useEffect* is run on every render of the component which we do not want since this will call *retrieveMovies* and *retrieveRatings* multiple times unnecessarily. We will later revisit *useEffect* to be called whenever the state changes.

```
const retrieveMovies = () =>{
  MovieDataService.getAll()
    .then(response =>{
      console.log(response.data)
      setMovies(response.data.movies)
    })
    .catch( e =>{
      console.log(e)
    })
}
```

retrieveMovies calls *MovieDataService.getAll()* which if you remember, has the following implementation:

```
getAll(page = 0){
  return http.get(`
    localhost://localhost:5000/api/v1/movies?page=${page}`
  )
}
```

getAll returns a promise with the movies retrieved from the database and we set it to the *movies* state variable with *setMovies(response.data.movies)*.

```
const retrieveRatings = () =>{
  MovieDataService.getRatings()
    .then(response =>{
      console.log(response.data)
      setRatings(["All Ratings"].concat(response.data))
    })
    .catch( e =>{
      console.log(e)
    })
}
```

In a similar fashion, *retrieveRatings* calls *MovieDataService.getRatings* to get the list of distinct ratings from the database. We however concat the response data to the *["All Ratings"]* array. In case the user doesn't specify any search criteria in the 'ratings' drop down menu, it will be set to 'All Ratings'.

Creating the Search Form

Now, let's get down to creating the search movies form where a user can search by title or ratings. We will first implement the below two methods, *onChangeSearchTitle* and *onChangeSearchRating*. So add it to the bottom of *movies-list.js*:

```
const onChangeSearchTitle = e => {
  const searchTitle = e.target.value
  setSearchTitle(searchTitle);
}

const onChangeSearchRating = e => {
  const searchRating = e.target.value
  setSearchRating(searchRating);
}
```

onChangeSearchTitle will be called whenever a user types into the search title field. *onChangeSearchTitle* will then take the entered value and set it to the component state. *onChangeSearchRating* works in the same fashion.

Form JSX Markup

Now, let's get the JSX for a simple form from the React bootstrap site (https://react-bootstrap.netlify.app/components/forms/) and put it into *movies-list.js*. It will look something like:

```
import ...
import Form from 'react-bootstrap/Form';
import Button from 'react-bootstrap/Button';
import Col from 'react-bootstrap/Col';
import Row from 'react-bootstrap/Row';
import Container from 'react-bootstrap/Container';

const MoviesList= props => {

  ...

  return (
    <div className="App">
      <Container>
        <Form>
          <Row>
            <Col>
              <Form.Group>
                <Form.Control
                  type="text"
                  placeholder="Search by title"
                  value={searchTitle}
                  onChange={onChangeSearchTitle}
                />
              </Form.Group>
              <Button
                variant="primary"
                type="button"
                onClick={findByTitle}
              >
                Search
              </Button>
            </Col>
            <Col>
              <Form.Group>
                <Form.Control
```

```
          as="select" onChange={onChangeSearchRating} >
          {ratings.map(rating =>{
            return(
              <option value={rating}>{rating}</option>
            )
          })}
        </Form.Control>
      </Form.Group>
      <Button
          variant="primary"
          type="button"
          onClick={findByRating}
        >
          Search
        </Button>
      </Col>
    </Row>
  </Form>
 </Container>
 </div>
 );
}
```

* Alternatively, you can refer to my source code for the above

Code Explanation

This creates a simple React form with a search by title field and search by ratings dropdown. We have used *Row* and *Col* to put the two search fields in a single row and in side by side columns (fig. 1).

Movie Reviews   Movies   Login

Search by title		All Ratings
Search		Search

Figure 1

Note that you have to import the *Form, Button, Container, Col* and *Row* components to use them.

```
      <Form.Group>
        <Form.Control
          type="text"
          placeholder="Search by title"
```

```
    value={searchTitle}
    onChange={onChangeSearchTitle}
  />
</Form.Group>
```

In the *searchTitle* FormControl, we set the field's value to the *searchTitle* state variable. So this field will always reflect the value in *searchTitle*. And we set *onChange* to *onChangeSearchTitle*, so any value changes done by the user entering in the field will call *onChangeSearchTitle* which will in turn update *searchTitle* state variable. In essence, we have double binded this field to the *searchTitle* state.

```
<Button
  variant="primary"
  type="button"
  onClick={findByTitle}
>
  Search
</Button>
```

The *search* Button calls the *findByTitle* method which we will implement later.

```
<Form.Group>
  <Form.Control
    as="select" onChange={onChangeSearchRating} >
    {ratings.map(rating =>{
      return(
        <option value={rating}>{rating}</option>
      )
    })}
  </Form.Control>
</Form.Group>
```

We then have *FormControl* which is the dropdown field to select a movie rating. To populate the option values for the dropdown, we use the *map* function, where for each *rating* in *ratings* array, we return an *option* element with the rating value for the select box (fig. 2).

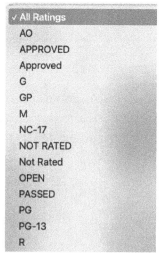

Figure 2

```
<Button
    variant="primary"
    type="button"
    onClick={findByRating}
>
  Search
</Button>
```

The *search* Button for the rating dropdown calls the *findByRating* method which we will implement later.

JSX Markup for Displaying Movies

Now, let's display the list of movies like in figure 3.

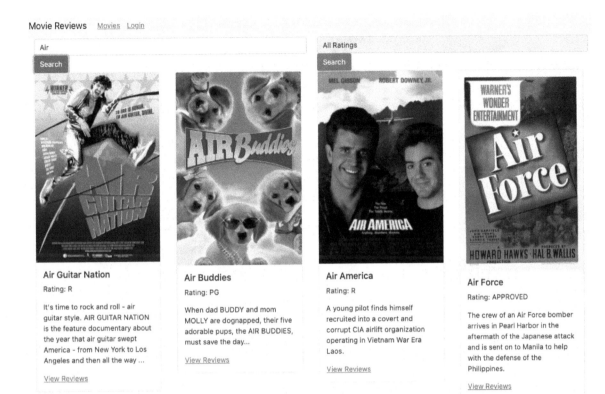

Figure 3

Add the code in **bold** below to *return*:

```
...
import Card from 'react-bootstrap/Card';

...

  return (
    <div className="App">
      <Container>
        <Form>
            ...
        </Form>

        <Row>
          {movies.map((movie) =>{
            return(
              <Col>
```

103

```
                    <Card style={{ width: '18rem' }}>
                      <Card.Img src={movie.poster+"/100px180"} />
                      <Card.Body>
                        <Card.Title>{movie.title}</Card.Title>
                        <Card.Text>
                          Rating: {movie.rated}
                        </Card.Text>
                        <Card.Text>{movie.plot}</Card.Text>
                        <Link to={"/movies/"+movie._id} >View Reviews</Link>
                      </Card.Body>
                    </Card>
                  </Col>
              )
            })}
          </Row>
        </Container>
      </div>
  );
```

Code Explanation

We use the *map* function again where for each movie in *movies*, we return a *Card* component which we take from React-bootstrap (https://react-bootstrap.github.io/components/cards/ - fig. 4).

Air Buddies

Rating: PG

When dad BUDDY and mom
MOLLY are dognapped, their five
adorable pups, the AIR BUDDIES,
must save the day...

View Reviews

Figure 4

Each Card contains one movie with its:
- poster image: `<Card.Img src={movie.poster+"/100px180"} />`,
- title: `<Card.Title>{movie.title}</Card.Title>`
- rating: `<Card.Text>Rating: {movie.rated} </Card.Text>`
- plot: `<Card.Text>{movie.plot}</Card.Text>`
- "View Reviews" Link: `<Link to={"/movies/"+movie._id} >View Reviews</Link>`

You can view all of the movie's properties back in MongoDB Atlas (fig. 5).

```
_id: ObjectId("573a1390f29313caabcd4135")
plot: "Three men hammer on an anvil and pass a bottle of beer around."
> genres: Array
  runtime: 1
> cast: Array
  num_mflix_comments: 1
  title: "Blacksmith Scene"
  fullplot: "A stationary camera looks at a large anvil with a blacksmith behind it..."
> countries: Array
  released: 1893-05-09T00:00:00.000+00:00
> directors: Array
  rated: "UNRATED"
> awards: Object
  lastupdated: "2015-08-26 00:03:50.133000000"
  year: 1893
> imdb: Object
  type: "movie"
> tomatoes: Object
```

Figure 5

Next, let's implement the *findByTitle* and *findByRating* functions.

findByTitle and findByRating functions

Add the following functions into *movies-list.js*:

```javascript
const find =(query, by) =>{
  MovieDataService.find(query,by)
    .then(response =>{
      console.log(response.data)
      setMovies(response.data.movies)
    })
    .catch(e =>{
      console.log(e)
    })
}
const findByTitle = () => {
  find(searchTitle, "title")
}
const findByRating = () => {
  if(searchRating === "All Ratings"){
    retrieveMovies()
  }
  else{
    find(searchRating, "rated")
  }
```

```
}
```

Code Explanation

```
const find =(query, by) =>{
  MovieDataService.find(query,by)
    .then(response =>{
      console.log(response.data)
      setMovies(response.data.movies)
    })
    .catch(e =>{
      console.log(e)
    })
}
```

The *find* function is supported by the *findByTitle* and *findByRating* methods. *find* simply provides the search query value entered by the user and by which field to search (i.e. *title* or *rated*) to *MovieDataService.find*:

```
find(query, by = "title", page = 0){
  return axios.get(
    `http://localhost:5000/api/v1/movies?${by}=${query}&page=${page}`
  )
}
```

find() in turn calls the backend API.

```
const findByTitle = () => {
  find(searchTitle, "title")
}
```

findByTitle is called by the 'Search by title's search button. It provides the title value to be searched to *find()* and tells it to search by 'title'.

```
const findByRating = () => {
  if(searchRating === "All Ratings"){
    retrieveMovies()
  }
  else{
    find(searchRating, "rated")
  }
}
```

107

findByRating is called by the 'Search by rating's search button. It provides the rating value to be searched to *find()* and tells it to search by 'rated'. However, if the user did not specify any rating value, the search value defaults to "All Ratings" and simply retrieves all movies.

Testing your App

When you run your app now, it should return a list of movies (fig. 6):

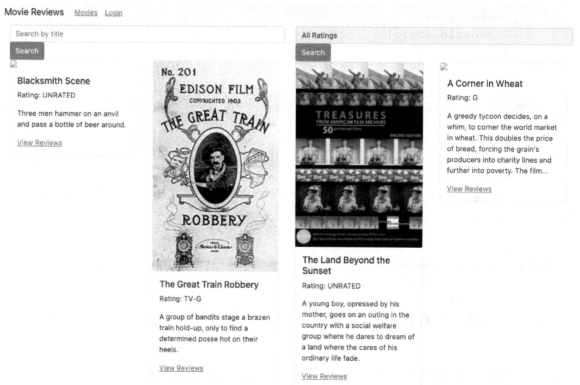

Figure 6

Try entering search terms in 'Search by title' or 'Search by rating' and it will return the related results (fig. 7, 8)! Note that some movies do not have a poster image.

train

All Ratings

Search

Search

Atomic Train

Rating: PG-13

A train filled with atomic devices
threatens to destroy the city of
Denver. John Serger (a train buff)
has to prevent this from happening

View Reviews

Last Train to Freo

Rating:

Two thugs from the Perth suburb
of Midland catch the last train to
Fremantle. When a young woman
boards the train a few stops later,
they begin talking and find out not
everyone on the train is who they
seem to be.

View Reviews

The Train

Rating: UNRATED

In 1944, a German colonel loads a
train with French art treasures to
send to Germany. The Resistance
must stop it without damaging the
cargo.

View Reviews

Figure 7 - Results for search by title: 'train'

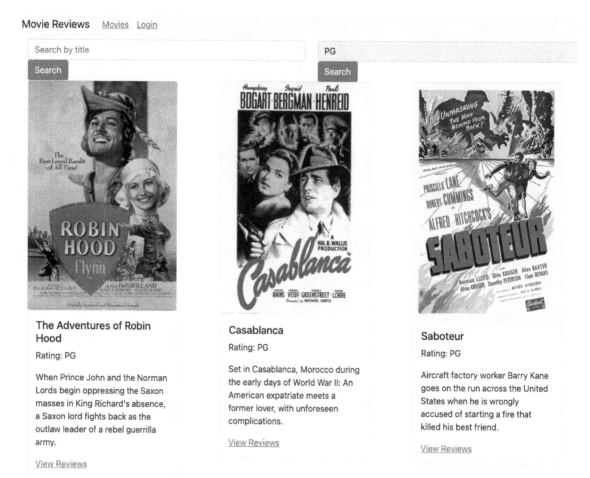

Figure 8 - Results for search by rating: 'PG'

Currently, we are displaying just the first twenty results. Later on, we will consider how to retrieve the next page's results. Now, let's carry on with viewing the reviews of a particular movie.

CHAPTER 18: MOVIE COMPONENT

Currently, when we click on 'View Reviews', it just shows a message. We will create a *Movie* component which shows the individual movie along with its reviews.

In the *components* folder, in *movie.js*, fill in the following code:

```
import React, {useState, useEffect} from 'react'
import MovieDataService from '../services/movies'
import { Link } from 'react-router-dom'

const Movie = props => {

  const [movie, setMovie] = useState({
    id: null,
    title: "",
    rated:"",
    reviews:[]
  })

  const getMovie = id =>{
    MovieDataService.get(id)
      .then(response => {
        setMovie(response.data)
        console.log(response.data)
      })
      .catch(e =>{
        console.log(e)
      })
  }

  useEffect(()=>{
    getMovie(props.match.params.id)
  },[props.match.params.id])

  return (
    <div>
    </div>
  );
}
```

```
export default Movie;
```

Code Explanation

```
const [movie, setMovie] = useState({
  id: null,
  title: "",
  rated:"",
  reviews:[]
})
```

We have a *movie* state variable to hold the specific movie we are currently showing in the Movie component. We set its initial values to null, empty strings ("") or an empty array *[]*.

```
const getMovie = id =>{
  MovieDataService.get(id)
    .then(response => {
      setMovie(response.data)
      console.log(response.data)
    })
    .catch(e =>{
      console.log(e)
    })
}
```

The *getMovie* method calls *get()* of *MovieDataService* (refer to chapter 16) which in turn calls the API route:

```
get(id){
    return axios.get(`http://localhost:5000/api/v1/movies/id/${id}`)
}
```

getMovie will be called by *useEffect*:

```
useEffect(()=>{
  getMovie(props.match.params.id)
},[props.match.params.id])
// won't call getMovie multiple times unless id is updated.
```

Remember that *useEffect* is called when the component renders. This time, however, we provide **props.match.params.id** into the second argument array. This means that *useEffect* should be called when the component first renders, and also each time the value of **props.match.params.id** (which holds that movie id) changes.

Thus, we avoid calling *getMovie* multiple times for the same movie id unless it is updated (which means we are displaying a different movie).

In essence, if the 2nd argument of *useEffect* contains an array of variables and any of these variables change, *useEffect* will be called.

To summarize:
useEffect without a second argument, is called each time a state change occurs in its body.
useEffect with an empty array in its second argument gets called only the first time the component renders.
useEffect with a state variable in the array gets called each time the state variable changes.

Now, where did we populate `props.match.params.id`?

Remember back in *App.js*, we have the *Route* for the *Movie* component:

```
<Route path="/movies/:id/" render={(props)=>
  <Movie {...props} user={user} />
}>
```

The route includes an *id* parameter for the movie id. So the route to get a specific movie will be something like: http://localhost:5000/movies/573a1390f29313caabcd6223

`props.match.params.id` will then give us *573a1390f29313caabcd6223*.

Movie Component Markup

Next, let's implement the frontend for the movie component. The frontend will look something like:

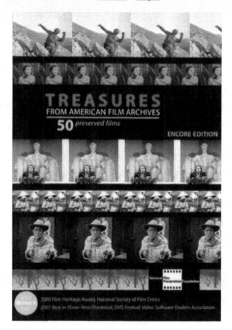

Movie Reviews   Movies   Login

The Land Beyond the Sunset

A young boy, opressed by his mother, goes on an outing in the country with a social welfare group where he dares to dream of a land where the cares of his ordinary life fade.

Add Review

Reviews

Figure 1

So in *components/movie.js*, import the following React-bootstrap components:

```
import Card from 'react-bootstrap/Card';
import Container from 'react-bootstrap/Container';
import Image from 'react-bootstrap/Image';
import Col from 'react-bootstrap/Col';
import Row from 'react-bootstrap/Row';
import Button from 'react-bootstrap/Button';
import Media from 'react-bootstrap/Media';
```

And fill in the below markup into the *return* method of *movie.js*:

```
return (
  <div>
    <Container>
      <Row>
        <Col>
          <Image src={movie.poster+"/100px250"} fluid />
        </Col>
```

```
        <Col>
          <Card>
            <Card.Header as="h5">{movie.title}</Card.Header>
            <Card.Body>
              <Card.Text>
                {movie.plot}
              </Card.Text>
              {props.user &&
              <Link to={"/movies/" + props.match.params.id + "/review"}>
                Add Review
              </Link>}
            </Card.Body>
          </Card>
          <br></br>
          <h2>Reviews</h2>
        </Col>
      </Row>
    </Container>
  </div>
);
```

Code Explanation

We essentially have two columns.

```
        ...
        <Col>
          <Image src={movie.poster+"/100px250"} fluid />
        </Col>
        <Col>
          <Card>
            ...
          </Card>
          ...
        </Col>
```

The first column contains the movie poster (if it exists) and the second column show the movie details in a Card component.

```
        {props.user &&
        <Link to={"/movies/" + props.match.params.id + "/review"}>
          Add Review
```

115

```
</Link>}
```

In the Card component, if the user is logged in, i.e. *props.user* is true, we include a link to 'Add Review' which we will implement later. Next, let's implement the listing of reviews.

CHAPTER 19: LISTING REVIEWS

We will be listing the reviews under the movie plot (fig. 1).

The Poor Little Rich Girl

Gwen's family is rich, but her parents ignore her and most of the servants push her around, so she is lonely and unhappy. Her father is concerned only with making money, and her mother ...

Add Review

Reviews

john reviewed on 2021-05-10T00:08:50.082Z

great movie

john reviewed on 2021-05-10T00:10:22.923Z

bad222 movie

jason reviewed on 2021-05-10T05:00:01.675Z

nice!

john reviewed on 2021-05-10T05:00:15.380Z

bad!

Figure 1

To do so, in *components/movie.js*, add the below mark up in **bold**:

```
<Container>
  <Row>
    ...
    <Col>
      <Card>
        ...
      </Card>
      <h2>Reviews</h2>
      <br></br>
      {movie.reviews.map((review, index)=>{
        return (
```

```
<Media key={index}>
  <Media.Body>
    <h5>{review.name + " reviewed on " + review.date}</h5>
    <p>{review.review}</p>
    {props.user && props.user.id === review.user_id &&
      <Row>
        <Col><Link to={{
          pathname:"/movies/"+
                    props.match.params.id+
                    "/review",
          state: {currentReview: review}
          }}>Edit</Link>
        </Col>
        <Col><Button variant="link">Delete</Button></Col>
      </Row>
    }
  </Media.Body>
</Media>
)
})}
</Col>
</Row>
</Container>
```

Code Explanation

We access the *reviews* array and using *map*, for each review, render a *Media* component from React-bootstrap (fig. 2).

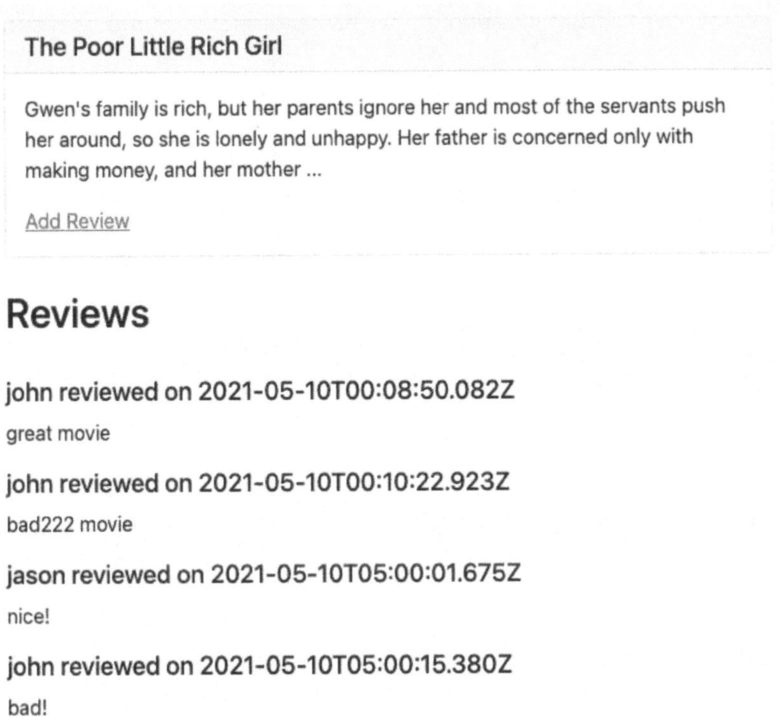

The Poor Little Rich Girl

Gwen's family is rich, but her parents ignore her and most of the servants push her around, so she is lonely and unhappy. Her father is concerned only with making money, and her mother ...

Add Review

Reviews

john reviewed on 2021-05-10T00:08:50.082Z

great movie

john reviewed on 2021-05-10T00:10:22.923Z

bad222 movie

jason reviewed on 2021-05-10T05:00:01.675Z

nice!

john reviewed on 2021-05-10T05:00:15.380Z

bad!

Figure 2

```
{props.user && props.user.id === review.user_id &&
  <Row>
    <Col><Link to={{
      pathname: "/movies/" + props.match.params.id +
                "/review",
      state: {currentReview: review}
    }}>Edit</Link></Col>
    <Col><Button variant="link">Delete</Button></Col>
  </Row>
}
```

A user can only delete reviews they have posted. They can't delete/edit other's reviews. Thus, we first check to see if a user is logged in (`props.user` is true). And only if the logged in user id is the same as the review user id (`props.user.id === review.user_id`), do we render the Edit/Delete buttons.

Testing our App

If you test your app, now, you will be able to go to a specific movie page and see its reviews. You won't

119

be able to see the Edit/Delete buttons at the moment because we have not implemented *login*. We will do that in the next chapter.

Formatting the Date

Before we go on to the next chapter, our current review date is in timestamp format e.g. *2021-05-10T00:08:50.082Z*. Let's format the review date(s) into a presentable manner. We will be using a library called *moment js*, a lightweight JavaScript library for parsing, validating and formatting dates.

In Terminal, in your project directory, install *moment js* with:

```
npm i moment --save
```

In *movie.js*, import moment with:

```
...
import moment from 'moment'

...
```

Then, pass your date format to the *moment* method:

```
<h5>
  {review.name+" reviewed on "} {moment(review.date).format("Do MMMM YYYY")}
</h5>
...
```

And when you run your app, the review dates should be nicely formatted (fig. 3).

Reviews

reviewed on 19th May 2021
123

reviewed on 19th May 2021
456

123 reviewed on 19th May 2021
acasc

Figure 3

CHAPTER 20: LOGIN COMPONENT

We won't be doing a full feature authentication system in this section, but it serves as a template for you to fill in your own full-fledged authentication implementation.
Fill in *login.js* with the following code:

```
import React, {useState} from 'react'
import Form from 'react-bootstrap/Form';
import Button from 'react-bootstrap/Button';

const Login = props => {

  const [name, setName] = useState("")
  const [id, setId] = useState("")

  const onChangeName = e => {
    const name = e.target.value
    setName(name);
  }

  const onChangeId = e => {
    const id = e.target.value
    setId(id);
  }

  const login = () => {
    props.login({name: name, id: id})
    props.history.push('/')
  }

  return(
    <div>
      <Form>
        <Form.Group>
          <Form.Label>Username</Form.Label>
          <Form.Control
            type="text"
            placeholder="Enter username"
            value={name}
            onChange={onChangeName}
          />
```

```
      </Form.Group>
      <Form.Group>
        <Form.Label>ID</Form.Label>
        <Form.Control
          type="text"
          placeholder="Enter id"
          value={id}
          onChange={onChangeId}
        />
      </Form.Group>
      <Button variant="primary" onClick={login}>
        Submit
      </Button>
    </Form>
  </div>
  )
}


export default Login;
```

* Refer to the source code (www.greglim.co/p/mern) if you prefer to copy and paste

Code Explanation

```
const [name, setName] = useState("")
const [id, setId] = useState("")
```

We set the initial name and id to be empty strings (""). Our simple login form consists of a username and id fields. The *onChangeName* and *onChangeId* methods bind the field values to the *name* and *id* state variables. They work in a similar fashion to the form we have earlier implemented in *MoviesList*, so I won't explain further.

```
const login = () => {
  props.login({name: name, id: id})
  props.history.push('/')
}
```

When we click on the Submit button, it calls *login*. Notice that we call *props.login*. But who passes this *login* function into the Login component? If you recall in *App.js*, we have the following route:

```
<Route path="/login" render={(props)=>
```

```
    <Login {...props} login={login} />
  }>
```

And *login* is defined in *App.js* as:

```
async function login(user = null){
  setUser(user)
}
```

So, from the *Login* component, we call the *login* function in *App.js* and set *App*'s *user* state. We are thus then able to pass on the logged-in *user* to other components e.g. *AddReview, Movie*.

After login, we then redirect to the main page with `props.history.push('/')`.

Testing your App

In your app, try logging in. Go to a specific movie with reviews (refer back to chapter 11 on how to create reviews via Insomnia) and you will be able to see the Edit/Delete buttons for each review (fig. 1).

Figure 1

CHAPTER 21: ADDING AND EDITING REVIEWS

Now, let's go on to implement adding a review. When a user logs in, goes to a specific movie page and clicks 'Add Review' (fig. 1), we will render the *AddReview* component for the user to submit a review (fig. 2).

> **The Land Beyond the Sunset**
>
> A young boy, opressed by his mother, goes on an outing in the country with a social welfare group where he dares to dream of a land where the cares of his ordinary life fade.
>
> Add Review

Figure 1

Movie Reviews   Movies   Logout User

Create Review

Submit

Figure 2

We will also use the *AddReview* component to edit a review. That is, when a user clicks on the 'Edit' link on an existing review (fig. 3).

123 reviewed on 2021-05-21

good movie

Edit

Figure 3

When editing, we will render the *AddReview* component but with the header 'Edit Review' (fig. 4). The existing review text will be shown where users can then edit and submit.

Figure 4

So, our *AddReview* component will allow us to both add and edit reviews. Let's first go through the code to add a review.

Adding a Review

In *add-review.js*, fill in the following code:

```
import React, { useState } from 'react'
import MovieDataService from "../services/movies"
import { Link } from "react-router-dom"
import Form from 'react-bootstrap/Form';
import Button from 'react-bootstrap/Button';

const AddReview = props => {

  let editing = false
  let initialReviewState = ""

  const [review, setReview] = useState(initialReviewState)
  // keeps track if review is submitted
  const [submitted, setSubmitted] = useState(false)

  const onChangeReview = e => {
    const review = e.target.value
    setReview(review);
  }

  const saveReview = () => {
    var data = {
      review: review,
      name: props.user.name,
      user_id: props.user.id,
```

```
        movie_id: props.match.params.id // get movie id direct from url
    }

    MovieDataService.createReview(data)
      .then(response => {
        setSubmitted(true)
      })
      .catch(e =>{
        console.log(e);
      })
  }

  return(
    <div>
      {submitted ? (
        <div>
          <h4>Review submitted successfully</h4>
          <Link to={"/movies/"+props.match.params.id}>
            Back to Movie
          </Link>
        </div>
      ):(
        <Form>
          <Form.Group>
            <Form.Label>{editing ? "Edit" : "Create"} Review</Form.Label>
            <Form.Control
              type="text"
              required
              value={review}
              onChange={onChangeReview}
            />
          </Form.Group>
          <Button variant="primary" onClick={saveReview}>
            Submit
          </Button>
        </Form>
      )}
    </div>
  )
}

export default AddReview;
```

* Refer to the source code (www.greglim.co/p/mern) if you prefer to copy and paste

Code Explanation

```
let editing = false
let initialReviewState = ""

const [review, setReview] = useState(initialReviewState)
const [submitted, setSubmitted] = useState(false)
```

The *editing* Boolean variable will be set to true if the component is in 'Editing' mode. False means we are adding a review.

We have a *review* state variable set to `initialReviewState`. In edit mode, `initialReviewState` will be set to the existing review text.

We also have a *submitted* state variable to keep track if the review is submitted.

```
const onChangeReview = e => {
  const review = e.target.value
  setReview(review);
}
```

The *onChangeReview* keeps track of the user-entered review value in the field:

```
            <Form.Control
              type="text"
              required
              value={review}
              onChange={onChangeReview}
            />
```

This should be familiar to you as we have used this a few times.

```
const saveReview = () => {
  var data = {
    review: review,
    name: props.user.name,
    user_id: props.user.id,
    movie_id: props.match.params.id // get movie id direct from url
  }
```

```
MovieDataService.createReview(data)
  .then(response => {
    setSubmitted(true)
  })
  .catch(e =>{
    console.log(e);
  })
}
```

saveReview is called by the submit button's **onClick={saveReview}**. In *saveReview*, we first create a *data* object containing the review's properties, e.g. the review text, user name etc.

```
name: props.user.name,
user_id: props.user.id,
```

We get *name* and *user_id* from props as this is passed into the *AddReview* component back in *App.js*:

```
<Route path="/movies/:id/review" render={(props)=>
  <AddReview {...props} user={user} />
}>
```

We get movie_id (**movie_id: props.match.params.id**) direct from the url back in *movie.js*:

```
<Link to={"/movies/" + props.match.params.id + "/review"}>
  Add Review
</Link>
```

We then call **MovieDataService.createReview(data)** which we implemented earlier in *movie.js* with the following code:

```
createReview(data){
  return axios.post("http://localhost:5000/api/v1/movies/review", data)
}
```

This then routes to *ReviewsController* in our backend and calls **apiPostReview** which then extracts *data* from the request's *body* parameter.

```
import ReviewsDAO from '../dao/reviewsDAO.js'

export default class ReviewsController{
  static async apiPostReview(req,res,next){
```

```
        try{
            const movieId = req.body.movie_id
            const review = req.body.review
            const userInfo = {
                name: req.body.name,
                _id: req.body.user_id
            }
...
```

Hopefully, you can see better how the whole flow in a MERN stack works now. Let's go on to implement editing a review.

Editing a Review

To have our *AddReview* component edit a review, add in two sections of code as shown below:

```
const AddReview = props => {

  let editing = false
  let initialReviewState = ""

  if(props.location.state && props.location.state.currentReview){
    editing = true
    initialReviewState = props.location.state.currentReview.review
  }

  const [review, setReview] = useState(initialReviewState)
  // keeps track is review is submitted
  const [submitted, setSubmitted] = useState(false)
      ...
      ...
      ...

  const saveReview = () => {
    var data = {
      review: review,
      name: props.user.name,
      user_id: props.user.id,
      movie_id: props.match.params.id // get movie id direct from url
    }
```

```
if(editing){
  // get existing review id
  data.review_id = props.location.state.currentReview._id
  MovieDataService.updateReview(data)
    .then(response =>{
      setSubmitted(true);
      console.log(response.data)
    })
    .catch(e =>{
      console.log(e);
    })
}
else{
  MovieDataService.createReview(data)
    .then(response => {
      setSubmitted(true)
      console.log(response.data)
    })
    .catch(e =>{
      console.log(e);
    })
}
}
```

Code Explanation

```
if(props.location.state && props.location.state.currentReview){
  editing = true
  initialReviewState = props.location.state.currentReview.review
}
```

We first check if a state is passed into *AddReview*. If you recall in *movie.js*, we pass in a state in the link to edit:

```
<Col><Link to={{
  pathname: "/movies/" + props.match.params.id + "/review",
  state: {
      currentReview: review
  }
}}>Edit</Link></Col>
```

Thus, in *AddReview*, we check if a state is passed in and contains a *currentReview* property. If so, set *editing* to true and the *initialReviewState* to *currentReview*'s review.

```
if(editing){
  // get existing review id
  data.review_id = props.location.state.currentReview._id
  MovieDataService.updateReview(data)
    .then(response =>{
      setSubmitted(true);
      console.log(response.data)
    })
    .catch(e =>{
      console.log(e);
    })
}
```

And if *editing* is true, we get the existing review id and call *updateReview* in *MovieDataService*.

```
updateReview(data){
  return axios.put("http://localhost:5000/api/v1/movies/review", data)
}
```

The above calls the *apiUpdateReview* method in *ReviewsController* in the backend similar to how we call *apiPostReview* for adding a review:

```
static async apiUpdateReview(req,res,next){
  try{
      const reviewId = req.body.review_id
      const review = req.body.review

    const date = new Date()

    const ReviewResponse = await ReviewsDAO.updateReview(
        reviewId,
        req.body.user_id,
        review,
        date
    )
    ...
```

If you recall, **apiUpdateReview** extracts the *movieId* and *review* text similar to what we have done in posting a review and then calls *updateReview* and pass in the user_id to ensure that the user who is updating the view is the one who has created it.

Running our App

Now, let's run our app. Login and go to a movie of your choice. Click on the 'Add Review' link and you should be able to add a review. The new review should appear in the movie page (fig. 5).

Figure 5

Having added the review, and if you are logged in, you will be able to edit the review by clicking on the 'Edit' link (fig. 6). And if you check your MongoDB, the data is updated there.

Figure 6

When you go back to your app and logout, you can't see the edit and delete buttons anymore. Next, we will finish up the implementation of deleting a review.

CHAPTER 22: DELETING A REVIEW

We are currently just rendering a delete button in the Movie component *movie.js*:

```
<Col>
  <Button variant="link">Delete
  </Button>
</Col>
```

Let's now implement its functionality by adding the below in **bold**:

```
<Col>
  <Button variant="link" onClick={() => deleteReview(review._id, index)}>
    Delete
  </Button>
</Col>
```

Next, add in the codes for *deleteReview* just above *return*:

```
const deleteReview = (reviewId, index) =>{
  MovieDataService.deleteReview(reviewId, props.user.id)
    .then(response => {
      setMovie((prevState) => {
        prevState.reviews.splice(index,1)
        return({
          ...prevState
        })
      })
    })
    .catch(e =>{
      console.log(e)
    })
}

return(
  ...
)
```

Code Explanation

```
<Button variant="link" onClick={() => deleteReview(review._id, index)}>
```

In the delete button, we pass in the review id and the index we got from the *movie.reviews.map* function into *deleteReview*.

In *deleteReview*, we then call *deleteReview* in *MovieDataService* which calls the delete API endpoint we implemented earlier:

```
deleteReview(id, userId){
  return axios.delete(
          `http://localhost:5000/api/v1/movies/review`,
          {data:{review_id: id, user_id: userId}}
  )
}
```

Remember that the *delete* endpoint is supported by *apiDeleteReview* in *ReviewsController* in the backend:

```
    static async apiDeleteReview(req,res,next){
        try{
            const reviewId = req.body.review_id
            const userId = req.body.user_id

/* ensure user who is deleting the review is the one who has created the
review */
            const ReviewResponse = await ReviewsDAO.deleteReview(
                reviewId,
                userId,
            )
      ...
```

Back in *movie.js*, we then add a callback function that is called when *deleteReview* completes:

```
const deleteReview = (reviewId, index) =>{
    MovieDataService.deleteReview(reviewId, props.user.id)
      .then(response => {
        setMovie((currState) => {
          currState.reviews.splice(index,1)
```

136

```
   return({
      ...currState
   })
 })
})
...
```

In the callback, we get the *reviews* array in the current state. We then provide the *index* of the review to be deleted to the *splice* method to remove that review. We then set the updated *reviews* array as the state.

Running your App

When you run your app now, log in and go to a specific movie, a user will be able to delete reviews they have posted. We have almost completed the entire functionality of our app using the MERN stack. What's left are some minor improvements to our app. Let's first see how to get the next page's results in the next chapter.

CHAPTER 23: GET NEXT PAGE'S RESULTS

Currently, we show just the first twenty results. We will add a 'Get next 20 results' link at the bottom to retrieve the next page's result (fig. 1).

Spider-Man

Rating: PG-13

When bitten by a genetically modified spider, a nerdy, shy, and awkward high school student gains spider-like abilities that he eventually must use to fight evil as a superhero after tragedy befalls his family.

View Reviews

Twelfth Night or What You Will

Rating: PG

Shakespeare's comedy of gender confusion, in which a girl disguises herself as a man to be near the count she adores, only to be pursued by the woman he loves.

View Reviews

Showing page: 0.   Get next 20 results

Figure 1

Our code in the backend has already made it easy for us to retrieve results by page. If you recall, in *MovieDataService*, we have:

```
getAll(page = 0){
  return axios.get(`https://localhost:5000/api/v1/movies?page=${page}`)
}
    ...
find(query, by = "title", page = 0){
  return axios.get(
    `https:// localhost:5000/api/v1/movies?${by}=${query}&page=${page}`
  )
}
```

This allows us to retrieve the results of a particular page by providing the page argument. This is supported by *MoviesDAO* in the backend, where we have:

```
cursor = await movies.find(query).limit(moviesPerPage).skip(moviesPerPage
```

```
* page)
```

to retrieve the results of a particular page by providing *moviesPerPage* and *page*.

Getting of Next Results for *getAll*

Let's first implement the getting of next results for *getAll*. That is, when a user doesn't specify any search query and just visits the home page.

In our *MoviesList* component *movies-list.js*, add the following in **bold**:

```
...
const MoviesList= props => {

  const [movies, setMovies] = useState([])
  const [searchTitle, setSearchTitle] = useState("")
  const [searchRating, setSearchRating] = useState("")
  const [ratings, setRatings] = useState(["All Ratings"])

  const [currentPage, setCurrentPage] = useState(0)
  const [entriesPerPage, setEntriesPerPage] = useState(0)

  useEffect(() =>{
    retrieveMovies()
    retrieveRatings()
  },[])

  useEffect(() =>{
    retrieveMovies()
  },[currentPage])

  const retrieveMovies = () =>{
    MovieDataService.getAll(currentPage)
      .then(response =>{
        setMovies(response.data.movies)
        setCurrentPage(response.data.page)
        setEntriesPerPage(response.data.entries_per_page)
      })
      .catch( e =>{
        console.log(e)
      })
  }
```

...

And in *return()*, add:

```
return (
    <div className="App">
      <Container>
        <Form>
        ...
        </Form>

          <Row>
            {movies.map((movie) =>{
            ...
            })}
          </Row>
          <br />
          Showing page: {currentPage}.
          <Button
            variant="link"
            onClick={() => {setCurrentPage(currentPage + 1)}}
          >
            Get next {entriesPerPage} results
          </Button>
      </Container>
    </div>
  );
```

Code Explanation

```
const [currentPage, setCurrentPage] = useState(0)
const [entriesPerPage, setEntriesPerPage] = useState(0)
```

We declare two state variables, *currentPage* (to keep track of which page we are currently displaying) and *entriesPerPage*. The two state variables are being populated in *retrieveMovies*:

```
const retrieveMovies = () =>{
  MovieDataService.getAll(currentPage)
    .then(response =>{
      setMovies(response.data.movies)
      setCurrentPage(response.data.page)
```

```
        setEntriesPerPage(response.data.entries_per_page)
    })
    .catch( e =>{
      console.log(e)
    })
  }
```

Remember that the JSON object returned from calling *MovieDataService.getAll* includes the properties *page* and *entries_per_page* (fig. 2):

```
{
  "movies": [ ↤ 20 ↦ ],
  "page": 0,
  "filters": {},
  "entries_per_page": 20,
  "total_results": 23530
}
```

Figure 2

Importantly, note that we provide the *currentPage* argument to *MovieDataService.getAll(**currentPage**)* to get results for that particular page.

We then add an *useEffect* hook:

```
  useEffect(() =>{
    retrieveMovies()
  },[currentPage])
```

Because we specified *currentPage* in the 2nd argument array, each time *currentPage* changes in value, this *useEffect* will be trigged and call *retrieveMovies* with the updated *currentPage* value.

```
        Showing page: {currentPage}.
        <Button
          variant="link"
          onClick={() => {setCurrentPage(currentPage + 1)}}
        >
          Get next {entriesPerPage} results
        </Button>
```

Finally, in *return*, we show *currentPage* to the user and provide a link button that displays "Get next ... results". When the link is clicked, it increments *currentPage* state variable and thus triggers *useEffect* and

142

calls *retrieveMovies*.

With this, we have implemented getting of next page's result for *getAll*. Now what about getting the next page's result when a user retrieves movies using search by title or search by rating? Let's implement it in the next chapter.

CHAPTER 24: GET NEXT PAGE'S RESULTS — SEARCH BY TITLE AND RATING

Our *MoviesList* component currently has two modes of retrieval. One is by calling *getAll*. The other is using *find()*. We have implemented getting next page's results for *getAll*. To do the same for *find*, we will first need another state variable to tell us which mode of retrieval a user is currently using. And whenever the user changes the retrieval mode, we will set *currentPage* back to page 0.

So, in *movies-list.js*, add the codes in **bold**:

```
...
const MoviesList= props => {
  ...
  const [currentPage, setCurrentPage] = useState(0)
  const [entriesPerPage, setEntriesPerPage] = useState(0)
  const [currentSearchMode, setCurrentSearchMode] = useState("")

  useEffect(() =>{
    setCurrentPage(0)
  },[currentSearchMode])

  useEffect(() =>{
    retrieveMovies()
    retrieveNextPage()
  },[currentPage])

  const retrieveNextPage = () => {
    if(currentSearchMode === "findByTitle")
      findByTitle()
    else if(currentSearchMode === "findByRating")
      findByRating()
    else
      retrieveMovies()
  }
  ...

  const find =(query, by) =>{
    MovieDataService.find(query,by,currentPage)
      .then(response =>{
        setMovies(response.data.movies)
```

```
    })
    .catch(e =>{
      console.log(e)
    })
  }
```

Code Explanation

```
const [currentSearchMode, setCurrentSearchMode] = useState("")

useEffect(() =>{
  setCurrentPage(0)
},[currentSearchMode])
```

We declare a new state variable *currentSearchMode* which contains the value either "", "findByTitle" or "findByRating".

We add a *useEffect* that whenever *currentSearchMode* changes, reset the *currentPage* to zero since it's a new search.

```
const retrieveNextPage = () => {
  if(currentSearchMode === "findByTitle")
    findByTitle()
  else if(currentSearchMode === "findByRating")
    findByRating()
  else
    retrieveMovies()
}
```

We have a new function *retrieveNextPage* which depending on the *currentSearchMode*, calls the relevant retrieval functions.

```
useEffect(() =>{
  retrieveMovies()
  retrieveNextPage()
},[currentPage])
```

We then change the current *useEffect* for *currentPage* to call *retrieveNextPage* instead of *retrieveMovies*.

```
const find =(query, by) =>{
  MovieDataService.find(query,by,currentPage)
```

And we add the *currentPage* argument to the call to *MovieDataService.find*.

Next, we have to set the current search mode in the various method calls.

Setting the Current Search Mode

In *retrieveMovies*, add:

```
const retrieveMovies = () =>{
  setCurrentSearchMode("")
  MovieDataService.getAll(currentPage)
    .then(response =>{
      ...
}
```

And in *findByTitle* and *findByRating*, add:

```
const findByTitle = () => {
  setCurrentSearchMode("findByTitle")
  find(searchTitle, "title")
}
const findByRating = () => {
  setCurrentSearchMode("findByRating")
  if(searchRating === "All Ratings"){
    retrieveMovies()
  }
  else{
    find(searchRating, "rated")
  }
}
```

With the above, our app can differentiate the current search mode. And if you run your app now, you will be able to retrieve the next page results successfully no matter which mode of retrieval you are using. What's next will be to deploy both the backend and frontend so that users can access it over the cloud. In the next chapter, we will do so for the backend.

CHAPTER 25: DEPLOYING BACKEND ON HEROKU

We have finished creating our entire app using the MERN stack. Now, we will show you how to deploy your backend to the web.

We will be deploying our Node.js backend to Heroku's servers to host and run on the Internet. The backend will connect to our cloud MongoDB Atlas database. The deployment process is relatively straightforward and you can simply follow along the instructions in the documentation to deploy Node.js apps on Heroku (https://devcenter.heroku.com/ - fig. 1).
But we will still walk you through the deployment process in this chapter.

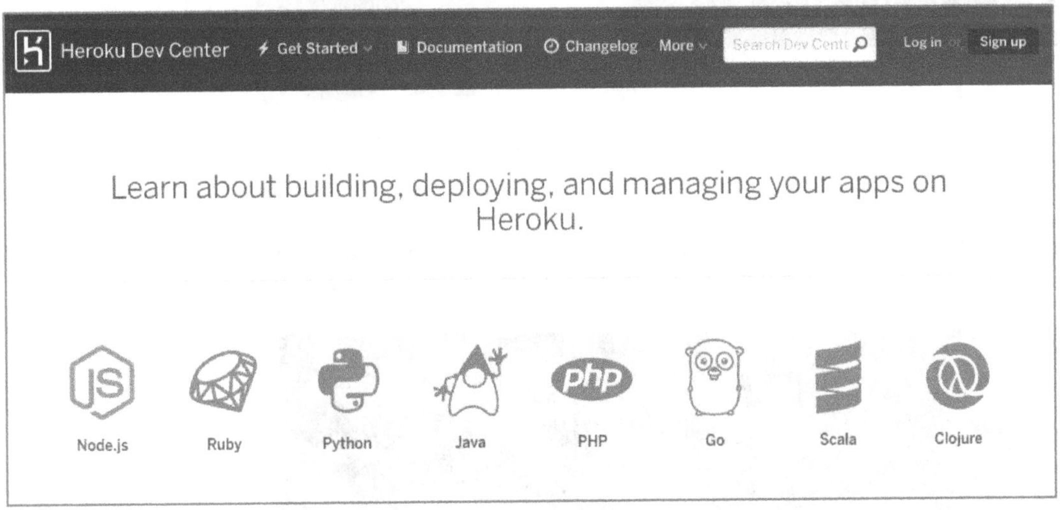

Figure 1

First, you will need a Heroku account. So, go ahead and sign up if you don't have an account.

Next, we need to install the Heroku Command Line Interface for creating and managing our Express apps on Heroku (fig. 2).

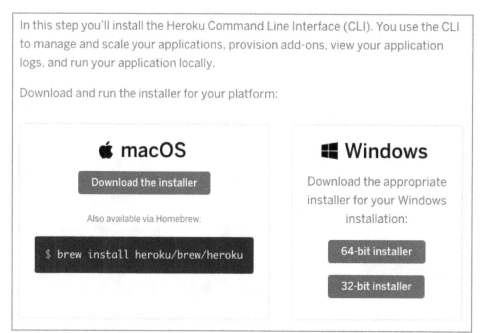

In this step you'll install the Heroku Command Line Interface (CLI). You use the CLI to manage and scale your applications, provision add-ons, view your application logs, and run your application locally.

Download and run the installer for your platform:

macOS

Download the installer

Also available via Homebrew:

$ brew install heroku/brew/heroku

Windows

Download the appropriate installer for your Windows installation:

64-bit installer

32-bit installer

Figure 2

When the installation completes, we can start using the *heroku* command from our Terminal. Type *heroku login* and a web browser will be opened to the Heroku login page (fig. 3).

```
$ heroku login
heroku: Press any key to open up the browser to login or q to exit
>    Warning: If browser does not open, visit
>    https://cli-auth.heroku.com/auth/browser/***
heroku: Waiting for login...
Logging in... done
Logged in as me@example.com
```

Figure 3

If the browser is already logged into Heroku, click 'Log In'.

Making our App 'Heroku Ready'

Before we start deploying to Heroku, we have to make our app 'Heroku ready'. We do so in the following sections by:
- adding a Procfile
- adding our Node.js version and *start* script to *package.json*
- listening on the correct port and

- specify the *.gitignore* file

Add a Procfile

In our app directory, create a file named *Procfile* (capital *P*, without a file extension). This file will be run when Heroku starts our app. In our simple app, this file will only be one line. Copy the below line into *Procfile*:

```
web: node index.js
```

web refers to the process type (the only process type that can receive HTTP traffic from the web). The command after *web* i.e. *node index.js* is run on the Heroku server.

package.json

Next, add the version of Node.js that your app requires in *package.json*. That is, find out the version of Node you are running using *node --version*, and add it to your *package.json*. Also add the *start* under "*scripts*" for Heroku to start our app via *index.js*.

An example is shown below in **bold**:

```
...
  "license": "MIT",
  "engines":{
    "node": "14.16.0"
  },
  "scripts": {
    "test": "echo \"Error: no test specified\" && exit 1",
    "start": "node index.js"
  },
  "author": "Start Bootstrap",
  "contributors": [
    "David Miller (http://davidmiller.io/)"
  ],
...
```

.gitignore

Next, if we have not already done so, create a file *.gitignore* in our app directory. This file tells Git to ignore whatever is specified in it from being pushed onto the server. And because we don't need to push *node_modules*, add **node_modules** to *.gitignore*

With these steps, our app is now 'Heroku ready' and we can go ahead to deploy our app.

Deployment

For deployment, if you haven't already, you need to have the *git* version control system installed. Install *git* by following the instructions in https://git-scm.com/book/en/v2/Getting-Started-Installing-Git and then setting up *git* for the first time (https://git-scm.com/book/en/v2/Getting-Started-First-Time-Git-Setup).

When *git* is installed and setup, set up a *git* project in the app's root directory with:

```
git init
```

Next, use:

```
git add .
```

to add all of our project files. Then to commit the changes to your Git project, run:

```
git commit -m "Initial commit"
```

You will see in the logs something like:

```
Created initial commit 5df2d09: My first commit
 44 files changed, 8393 insertions(+), 0 deletions(-)
 create mode 100644 README
 create mode 100644 Procfile
 create mode 100644 app/controllers/source_file
...
```

Next, run:

```
heroku create
```

This creates a new empty application on Heroku with an associated empty Git repository. A new URL for your Heroku app will also be setup (fig. 4).

```
remote: -----> Launching...
remote:        Released v4
remote:        https://guarded-savannah-47368.herokuapp.com/ deployed to Heroku
remote:
remote: Verifying deploy... done.
```
Figure 4

You can change the URL or associate a domain name you own with the Heroku address but it is beyond the scope of this book.

Now, we push our code to the remote Git repository that we have just created with:

```
git push heroku master
```

This will push the code to the Heroku servers and setup our app's dependencies on them. Going forward when there are code changes in our app, run `git push heroku master` again to re-deploy.

And if you go to the URL generated for you and append */api/v1/movies* e.g.:

https://guarded-savannah-47368.herokuapp.com/api/v1/movies/

you will see the movies' data results!

In other words, previously, you accessed the API on your local machine with http://localhost:5000/api/v1/movies for example. Now, you access it using the URL Heroku has generated for you. And you can stop the Node process running on your local machine.

Changes to Frontend React Code

After we deploy our frontend React code, we must ensure any requests we are sending from the client-side is changed to use our Heroku generated URL now instead of localhost. Thus, change the hostname in your React frontend, *movies.js* under *services* folder. E.g.

```
class MovieDataService{

  getAll(page = 0){
    return axios.get(`
        https://guarded-savannah-47368.herokuapp.com/api/v1/movies?page=${page}
    `)
  }
    ...
```

And also make sure that you are using *https* instead of just *http* as content must be served over secure *https*.

CHAPTER 26: HOSTING AND DEPLOYING OUR REACT FRONTEND

In this section, we will deploy our React frontend to the Internet to share it with the world. We are going to use Netlify (netlify.com – fig.1) for our deployment.

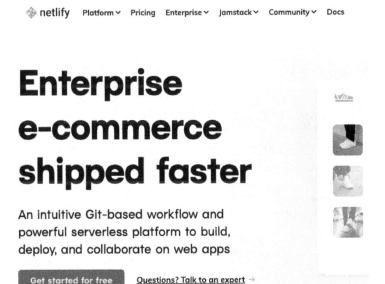

Figure 1

Go to netlify.com and create a free account or log in if you already have one.

When you log in, a list will show any deployed apps that you have. In your case, it will be empty since this is probably your first time deploying on Netlify. At the bottom, there will be a box with the message, "Want to deploy a new site without connecting to Git? Drag and drop your site output folder here" (fig. 2).

Want to deploy a new site without connecting to Git?
Drag and drop your site output folder here

Figure 2

Go back to the Terminal and navigate to the *frontend* folder. Build your React application with the command:

`npm run build`

This will create a build version of React that we can deploy on the web. When the build is finished, you will be able to see a *build* folder in the directory.

Select the *build* folder and drag and drop it into the box we saw earlier in Netlify. Netlify will take a few seconds and then generate a url where you can access the page (fig. 3).

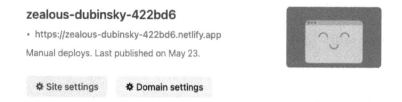

Figure 3

If you wish to have your own custom domain, you can go to 'Add custom domain' to purchase one.

And there you have it! Both your MERN frontend and backend are deployed to the app, meaning that your fully functioning MERN app is live and running.

Final Words

We have gone through quite a lot of content to equip you with the skills to create a MERN stack app.

Hopefully, you have enjoyed this book and would like to learn more from me. I would love to get your feedback, learning what you liked and didn't for us to improve.

Please feel free to email me at support@i-ducate.com to get updated versions of this book.

If you didn't like the book, or if you feel that I should have covered certain additional topics, please email us to let us know. This book can only get better thanks to readers like you.

If you like the book, I would appreciate if you could leave us a review too. Thank you and all the best for your learning journey in MERN stack development!

About the Author

Greg Lim is a technologist and author of several programming books. Greg has many years in teaching programming in tertiary institutions and he places special emphasis on learning by doing.

Contact Greg at support@i-ducate.com or http://www.greglim.co/

Printed in the USA
CPSIA information can be obtained
at www.ICGtesting.com
LVHW081630170923
758459LV00040B/452